# A PORTRAIT OF THE ARTIST AS A YOUNG GIRL

'I was extraordinarily lucky to be born into a family about whom I have nothing but warm memories and sad regrets that it can't still be there.' **Maeve Binchy**

'It was only when I wrote *All of Us There* that I discovered how happy I had been and how much loved I was in my childhood.' **Polly Devlin**

'My childhood certainly wasn't idyllic. There were certainly marvellous moments but there were also long, long periods of boredom.' **Molly Keane**

'All the interests, all the peculiarities and all the weaknesses I have were all there when I was a child.' **Dervla Murphy**

'I haven't lost my childhood and I hope I never will, because it is the fount and source of my writing.' **Edna O'Brien**

Formerly a teacher and an editor with an educational publisher, John Quinn is now a senior producer with the Education Department in RTE Radio, Ireland. *A Portrait of the Artist as a Young Girl* is based on his highly acclaimed series of interviews of that name, first heard on RTE Radio in the summer of 1985. He is married with three children and lives near Dublin.

# A PORTRAIT OF THE ARTIST AS A YOUNG GIRL

edited by John Quinn

*With a Foreword by Seamus Heaney*

A Methuen Paperback
in association with
Radio Telefís Éireann

*for Lisa, Deirdre and Declan*
*—artists all*

First published in Great Britain 1986
This paperback edition published 1987
by Methuen London Ltd,
11 New Fetter Lane, London EC4P 4EE
in association with
Radio Telefís Éireann, Dublin 4, Ireland
Copyright © Radio Telefís Éireann 1985
Introduction © John Quinn 1986
Foreword © Seamus Heaney 1986

Printed in Great Britain
by Richard Clay Ltd, Bungay, Suffolk

British Library Cataloguing in Publication Data

A Portrait of the artist as a young girl.
 1. Women authors, Irish—Anecdotes
 2. English fiction—Irish authors
 3. English fiction—Women authors
 I. Quinn, John
 823'.912'099287      PN471

 ISBN 0-413-14360-0

# Contents

---

List of Illustrations   vii

Acknowledgements   ix

Foreword   xi

Introduction   xiii

Maeve Binchy   1

Clare Boylan   17

Polly Devlin   33

Jennifer Johnston   49

Molly Keane   63

Mary Lavin   79

Joan Lingard   93

Dervla Murphy   111

Edna O'Brien   131

# *List of Illustrations*

———

1. The young Maeve Binchy.

2. Maeve Binchy.

3. Clare Boylan on her First Communion day.

4. Clare Boylan.

5. Four of the Devlin sisters as children:
(*left to right*) Polly, Marie, Val and Anne.

6. Polly Devlin.

7. The young Jennifer Johnston with her mother,
Shelah Richards – and friends.

8. Jennifer Johnston.

9. Molly Keane.

10. Mary Lavin.

11. The young Joan Lingard and her dog.

12. Joan Lingard.

13. Dervla Murphy with her bicycle.

14. Edna O'Brien.

# Acknowledgements

The editor is grateful to the following for permission to reproduce copyright material in this book:

Hamish Hamilton Ltd for excerpts from *Holy Pictures* by Clare Boylan and the excerpt from *The Captains and the Kings* by Jennifer Johnston;

Polly Devlin for excerpts from *All of Us There* published by Weidenfeld and Nicolson;

Andre Deutsch Ltd for excerpts from *Good Behaviour* by Molly Keane;

Constable Ltd for excerpts from 'Tom' in *The Shrine and Other Stories* by Mary Lavin;

David Higham Associates for excerpts from *Sisters by Rite* by Joan Lingard published by Hamish Hamilton (hardback) and Arrow Books (paperback);

John Murray (Publishers) Ltd for excerpts from *Wheels Within Wheels* by Dervla Murphy;

Edna O'Brien for excerpts from *The Country Girls*, *Mother Ireland* and *Returning* by Edna O'Brien published by Penguin Books.

Acknowledgements for photographic material are due to The RTE Guide, RTE Illustrations Library, Camera Press, The Irish Times, Joan Lingard, Maeve Binchy, Clare Boylan, Polly Devlin and Jennifer Johnston.

Thanks also to the RTE Stills Department for photographic work, to Mary Burke who typed the original interview transcripts and very special thanks to Anne Askwith of Methuen for her courtesy, efficiency and many helpful suggestions in preparing the manuscript for publication.

# Foreword

The chapters of this book are edited versions of interviews conducted by John Quinn who produced and presented the original series of radio programmes entitled *A Portrait of the Artist as a Young Girl* in 1985. This is an important consideration, because it means that the book presents us with writers talking rather than writers composing; there is an off-the-cuff immediacy in much of what is said; it is first rather than second thoughts that we are reading. There is, consequently, good lively delivery of facts and memories, with nothing of that studied languorous note which can easily creep in when the subject of childhood is addressed.

When they talk about their childhoods, writers come close to the centre of the mystery they are to themselves. Most novelists and poets can, of course, give a reasonable account of how and why they got launched on their careers; yet that account is in itself an invention of sorts, another exercise of their gift for telling stories and making images. But here the word 'invention' has no suggestion of faking or fabrication; rather, it reaches back to its old Latin meaning of discovery, and to its Renaissance association with creative imagination. The invention of a narrative for one's childhood is therefore to some extent a creative discovery of the self.

One of my own favourite inventions of this kind is William Wordsworth's image of the River Derwent as a maternal tongue which licked his poetic being into shape. The river ran past the end of the garden of the house where he was born in Cockermouth, and its noise flowed along his dreams and infused his infant attention with messages of the power and beauties of the natural world. If none of the contributors to this volume is as absolute (or vain) as Wordsworth in assuming that the whole cosmos was just waiting for her arrival to start ministering to her imagination, each one nevertheless has something individual and persuasive to add to that great deposit of evidence which shows childhood to be the great forcing house of artistic talent.

The woman writer, like everybody else, is in pursuit of coherence, attempting to bring into significant alignment the creature she was and the being she is striving to become. To use Keats's distinction, she is engaged in the process of schooling her intelligence into a soul. The mixture of self-knowledge and self-direction required for this task, the way in which concessions to innate temperament have to be balanced against the will towards change, the whole delicate and crucial negotiation between the unconscious and self-consciousness, between the deliberate and arbitrary – in the following pages, all of these things, which are a constant and usually unexamined feature of any life, come under good-natured and salutary scrutiny.

But I am making it all sound too heavy. There is a direct no-nonsense tone about what these women have to say; there is good variety; there is condensed social history and implicit domestic drama; there is all the energy which springs from commitment and fulfilment; and overall there is a nice political edge to the book, insofar as it constitutes a spirited displacement of the aura of maleness which still tends to surround that hallowed word, 'artist'.

Seamus Heaney

# Introduction

---

When Dylan Thomas declared that 'people had better be quick telling me about their childhood or I'll soon be telling them about mine' I'm not sure that he was expressing a commonly held feeling. Certainly when I approached the artists who are featured in this book with a view to doing a radio interview on their respective childhoods, the initial reactions were varied. There *were* those who were quick to tell me about their childhood; but there were also some who wondered if anyone would be interested in an 'ordinary' childhood (is any childhood ever ordinary?) and others who were somewhat bemused by my request because they had not previously delved publicly into their childhood.

It has often intrigued me that when writers or 'celebrities' of any kind are interviewed about their lives and careers, childhood is often dismissed in the opening minutes in favour of what is invariably far less interesting material. I therefore resolved that the radio series *A Portrait of the Artist as a Young Girl* (with apologies to Mr Joyce) would confine itself to childhood, to the people and the environment which shaped the adult lives of the artists; and with a little cajoling and a lot of persistence all of those approached agreed to be interviewed. The resulting series, first broadcast on RTE Radio in the summer of 1985, vindicated my feelings, both about the importance of childhood for the artists involved and the interest it would hold for a listening audience – indeed not least for the artists themselves who found it a surprisingly interesting experience.

When the suggestion was made that the interviews would make an interesting book, a very obvious difficulty arose. How do you transfer material, however interesting, from a medium which caters for the ear to one which caters for the eye? Radio and print are two very different media and what is successful in the one cannot be guaranteed to transfer successfully to the other. At the very least a lot of careful editing and re-ordering of material is required. I leave the reader to judge how successfully that has been done in this instance. In that sense, I am far more responsible than the artists involved for what is in the pages of this book.

Conversely, because radio and print are such different media there are things that one can do which the other cannot. If the writers featured in this book were each commissioned to *write* an essay on their childhood, it would be a very different book, but not necessarily, I would argue, a more interesting one. The studied essay would not, I feel, capture the spontaneity and the candour that the radio interview can generate. And if there is one thread that links the chapters of this book it is candour. For myself, interviewing these writers was a pleasure and editing the interviews into 'self-portraits' for this book was a further source of enjoyment. I hope the reader will derive equal enjoyment from the finished product.

John Quinn

# Maeve Binchy

———

Maeve Binchy was born in Dublin in 1940. She gave up her original career of teaching to become a columnist with the *Irish Times*, for which newspaper she still writes. Her first attempts at fiction were short-story collections, based on her acute observation of the people about her: *Central Line*, *Victoria Line* and *Dublin Four*. She has written a successful television play, *Deeply Regretted By*, but it is her two major novels, *Light a Penny Candle* and *Echoes*, which have established Maeve Binchy as a best-selling writer. She now lives in London.

I HAVE a very firm earliest memory. I, the first born, was three and a half and my mother was expecting another child. I was constantly asking God to send *me* a new brother or sister. The 'me' was important because I loved receiving parcels and presents that *I* could open. I was outraged when the baby arrived, because all the attention shifted from me to this small red-faced thing in a cot. It was a great disappointment to me. I had been praying for this moment; and now here was this 'thing', wailing and wailing, and everybody was saying how beautiful it was. 'Honestly', I said, 'I would have preferred a rabbit!' And I *would* have preferred a rabbit at that time because although my school pals had brothers and sisters I had wanted a rabbit for ages. For the next three years I wanted to send my sister back. When I think of the great friendship I have with her now I cringe at the thought of wanting to exchange her for a rabbit when I was three and a half years old.

Home was initially in Dun Laoghaire and later in Dalkey, Co. Dublin. I *love* Dalkey. It's not just a sentimental attachment – I just love the hills and the sea, and walking over Dalkey Hill along the Green Road in Killiney and down the Vico Road. Of course I got very used to walking as a child. I was the eldest of four so there was always somebody in a pram (never, alas, a rabbit!) to be wheeled out for a walk.

My father was William Binchy, a barrister who came from Charleville, Co. Cork. Although he never rose to higher than junior counsel he was very much respected by his colleagues. He loved the law; he would talk for hours on end about the rules of law to anyone who would listen, including his own children. He was particularly kind and helpful to young people who were studying law. My father was a very gentle man, never very socially outgoing; he wasn't a member of a golf club nor would he go out for a drink – but he loved talking about the law!

My mother was Maureen Blackmore, a nurse from Carrick-on-Suir, Co. Tipperary, and she was studying to be a physiotherapist when she met my father. She was the exact opposite to him in character. She was very lively and outgoing, and would talk to everybody and anybody about anything. Whereas my father was very much the intellectual and was always getting us to study for exams and to read, my mother thought *people* were all important. To any outsider they would have seemed totally unsuited to each other but, as my sisters and brother would tell you, it would be hard to find a couple who got on better together. They were extremely happy and were delighted with each other.

I can only remember one row that they had. We had rented a house in Ballybunion for the month of August – which was a great excitement in itself. One evening my parents had a simple difference of opinion about whether the shafts of the common cart went upwards or downwards. The whole thing was ridiculous – I suppose it depends on which way you put the cart – but it seemed to develop into a much bigger row as time went on. It was probably the kind of row that took place in many homes and which would pass over most children's heads like music on the radio; but to the four Binchys it was the first time that they had heard their parents raise their voices to each other and we were absolutely certain they were going to part. We sat on the stairs, planning our future. I would probably have to go with Daddy because he couldn't make the tea and Billy could come with me, too . . . The two girls could go with Mummy . . . It was very reassuring later that evening to hear the laughter which proclaimed that the row was over.

But that was an exceptional event. Generally ours was a warm and happy home. My mother was very protective of us – so much so that it was something of a family joke. There was one occasion I remember particularly. When I was at the convent school the nuns used to bring us down from the school for swims on Killiney beach and my mother kept wondering if the nuns would be sure to get Maeve properly dry after her swim, because it would be terrible if she put on damp clothes and caught rheumatic fever . . . I remember my father saying in a most exasperated tone, 'Maureen, why don't you take an electric fire down to the beach and warm the child when she comes out of the sea?'

My mother also had this view that, if she made our home a centre for lots of our friends to come to, then she would know where we all were and she would not have to worry about us; so our house became a centre, a meeting-point for children of all ages. My mother didn't have much of a home life when she was young: her parents had died when she was a child and she had been brought up by step-relations. I think that she tried to compensate for this by ensuring that her own family would be a very definite and important entity – and that was something she certainly realised for all of us. I know there is always a danger that you look back too sympathetically – rose-coloured spectacles and all that – but my childhood *was* a great joy. We were very much an entity. We all still lived together at an age when most people got out of the nest and went off to other places: we all lived at home when we went to university. Maybe if we had left earlier we might have been more independent but it was nice and it was good; and on a Saturday afternoon, when we used to bring all our friends back to our house, home was where the 'crack' was.

I was twenty-eight when my mother died, and thirty when my father died. For a woman of that age, I was absolutely bereft. Not only did I have to bear the loss of these two very great people but at my father's death my home ended too. Whereas most people have a life of their own by the age of thirty, I had none. I had been living at home up to then and I was totally bereft.

At the age of five I went to St Anne's, a lovely little nursery school in Clarinda Park in Dun Laoghaire. It was run by a Mrs Russell, who was one of those wonderful old women with white hair and a straight back that you always saw as somebody's grandmother in old films. She was terribly correct and very kind. There were two other ladies – her nieces, I think – both called Miss Bath. One was fat and one was thin; with typical childish cruelty we called them 'Hot Bath' and 'Cold Bath'. We didn't have a school uniform, but my great excitement was wearing a big bow on my head. The bow was ironed for me every morning and I went off to school looking like a cockatoo! I enjoyed my three years in St Anne's.

My next school was a convent school in Killiney, Co. Dublin, run by the Order of the Holy Child Jesus. These nuns had come to Ireland after the war. It was said that they had come at the invitation of the then Archbishop of Dublin, John Charles McQuaid, because he was terrified that too many middle-class Irish girls were going to convents in England, where they might do that dreadful thing: they might meet someone of a different faith and possibly threaten their own faith and be lost to us forever! I don't know whether all this was true or not, but that is what we always believed.

The nuns were terribly nice and very innocent. They were somewhat like the Somerville and Ross's *Irish R.M.* coming over here, because they really had no idea what they were about at all. One of them, whom I have met since, used to say that 'one was either sent to the Gold Coast or to Eire on one's missionary duty'. You got the feeling that the Gold Coast might have been a better bargain, because we used to tell them all a pack of lies. They didn't understand the Irish language or its pronunciation; nor did they understand the importance of Irish in the school curriculum. Consequently, the first year that the Leaving Certificate examination was taken in that school I think nearly every student failed Irish. Irish teachers were brought in before the next year in order to sort that problem out.

All my school reports said that I was bright but lazy: I didn't stir myself enough. I was lucky, in that my mind was quick. I could understand things quickly and then I would spend the rest of the time in a daydream. There were some things I was very poor at – mathematics I didn't understand at all, and I am still practically innumerate – but I was fortunate enough to be at the top of the class.

However, in those days being at the top of the class wasn't nearly as important as being good at games. To have big strong arms and be able to hit the hockey ball miles down the pitch – that was real status. I didn't enjoy games. We all wore green uniforms tied in the middle and we looked like potato sacks of various sizes. I remember standing on the hockey pitch, my legs blue with the cold, hoping that all the action would remain at the far end and that I would not be called on to do anything. I was a real thorn in the flesh for the unfortunate games mistress who had to deal with me: full of sulks, refusing to vault the horse or hit the ball in case I did myself an injury.

But I enjoyed netball. I was very tall, even at the age of fourteen, which led the games mistress to believe that I had great potential on the netball team as a shooter. She figured that I was so tall that even if I just stood there, dreaming of the future and thinking my own thoughts, when the ball came into my hands it would be as easy for me to put it into the net as it was to throw it away. I was a great success. I was in the 1st VII team for netball for two whole years, which was lovely because we went out to other convents on Wednesday afternoons to play netball, and we had tea and buns afterwards. We won all our games and a lot of the other schools protested, saying that I was too old and could not possibly be under fourteen. I was, to use the modern parlance, a lethal striker.

Apart from hockey, the other thing I hated – we *all* hated it – was being dragged to the beach by the nuns. They would say, 'Come on girls, show some school spirit.' It was very easy for them to say that when they had about nine thousand black petticoats on them and they didn't have to go into the icy sea and show school spirit.

One Christmas at school – I must have been about nine – there was great excitement because I won a prize in a magazine called *The Pylon* (as in electric pylon). It was a missionary magazine to aid the missionary effort of the Holy Child sisters. All of us who contributed 3*d*. a year (or whatever) were called

Electrons. The whole thing sounds ridiculous now; but then it was terribly important to save our money and enter competitions to keep up the good name of the school ('Show some school spirit, girls!'). One of the competitions was to write a story about the missions. I entered and won. I have never found my story since, but I remember my father saying to me as we were going home from school that day, 'When you become a writer, you will always be able to say *this* was your first work.' 'This' is now lost – mercifully, because I do remember that it was a story about Jane, who wanted to be a missionary and 'teach the fuzzy-wuzzy natives'! It's not something that I would necessarily be proud to put in any collection of my work. I think Jane did manage to teach the fuzzy-wuzzy natives, who were all beaten out of their own ways and brought around to our ways – and so my prize-winning story 'ended happily'. I was a *very* good Electron.

My father always encouraged us to read. He had a study where he kept all his law books; but he had quite a collection of other books, many of which he bought in the second-hand bookshops along the quays on his way back from the Four Courts. My mother was not a great reader, although she liked novels and read quite a few of them, but she loved going to auctions and she would buy trays and boxes full of books. As a result we had an awful lot of books at home, and I was very lucky to grow up in such a house of books. Of course, as a teenager I always felt that when your parents advised you to do something you should resist it as much as possible, so when my father used to tell me to read Carlyle, Trollope and Thackeray I resisted as far as possible. It was only when I reached late teens that I started to read them and I began to think that they were good, in spite of being recommended.

I left Enid Blyton at an early age and got into Peter Cheyney and Agatha Christie. I read Graham Greene, also at an early age. I remember *Stamboul Train* being taken very, very firmly from me. I would ask innocent questions like, 'Why was there such a fuss over his spending the night in her cabin on the train? Weren't there two berths there?' My parents decided that my reading matter was a little too 'adult'.

Apart from books, I loved the radio. I always associate Saturday nights in my childhood with *Saturday Night Theatre* on the radio. Being the eldest, I was allowed to stay up for *Saturday Night Theatre*. I have never written a radio play but I have always loved listening to radio plays. I agree with the boy who said that he preferred radio to television because the pictures were better.

I wanted to be a saint. This was not just a childhood ambition: I wanted to be a saint until I was about twenty-two. It wasn't a question of 'I hope it will happen to me'; I was quite convinced that I would be a saint.

I had a very special relationship with God. I regarded him as a friend, and Irish, and somebody who knew me well. He had sent particular tortures my way – like not being good at games (until the marvellous netball 'discovery') and being fat at school. It was bad, very bad, to be fat, so these were the tortures that God was sending to try me. It was all very clear to me.

But I was hoping against hope that I wouldn't see a vision. People who saw visions very often ended up as martyrs; and although I was dead keen to be a saint, I wanted to be a non-martyred saint. Because of all the stories I had heard about the children of Fatima seeing Our Lady in a tree I always kept my eyes down on the road if I was walking anywhere with lots of trees. No visions for me! I had worked out this sainthood very well. You didn't have to be a martyr; you didn't even have to be a nun and devote your whole life to sanctity. You just had to have a special relationship with God and be a sort of intermediary between Him and the rest of the world.

I worried a lot about people who didn't keep up their own religion. I had a friend whose father was a Protestant – a lovely man whom we all adored because he used to give us fourpenny ice-creams when every other father only gave us twopenny ones. He used to drive his wife and children to Mass and then go for a walk on Dun Laoghaire pier. I would spend hours with his daughter wondering if he would be damned and roasted in hell. I felt that if he wasn't converted to Catholicism (which would be the ideal thing) he should at least be going to his own church (which would naturally not be as good as the *real* thing). Imagine this poor unfortunate man being harangued by his eight-year-old daughter and her friend saying, 'Honestly, Mr —, have you thought about it – the devil and the pain that goes on forever?' The more I look back on it, the more I realise what a poisonous little person I was – and having an over-developed imagination didn't help.

Part of the sainthood thing, too, was becoming a Child of Mary. This involved a combination of being in a sodality – a religious group – and being a prefect in school. You couldn't become a Child of Mary unless your peers and the nuns said that you were a person of great worth, high leadership quality and all the rest of it. I went off on my own to do a one-day retreat and then on 8 December I was made a Child of Mary. It was a lovely ceremony with candles all around, and I wore a veil and a big blue ribbon with the Child of Mary medal on it. I was bursting with awareness of the importance of it all and always wore this big ribbon on my plump green chest.

But it was not to last. A very short time afterwards I was stripped of the medal, just like a soldier is cashiered from the army by having his buttons cut off. It happened like this. Most of the boarders had boyfriends. I didn't have any, but I became very popular by volunteering to post the boarders' letters to their boyfriends. I used to stuff the letters down the front of my gymslip and smuggle them out for posting. One evening, I was accosted by a nun, who kept talking to me and asking me if I was all right, because I looked as if I were dying of angina, clutching my chest. 'Oh, I'm fine, Mother, fine,' I blurted out, as one by one the letters slipped from under my gymslip. It was so humiliating as the nun picked up the letters addressed to Master Sean O'Brien, Master John Smith and so on. I really felt that the pit of hell was opening up in front of me.

'Isn't it very sad my dear,' she said icily, 'that you are not a person to be trusted? Tomorrow morning at assembly you will give your medal back.'

And so it was that, red-eyed, I handed back my Child of

Mary medal. It was a bitter disappointment, particularly in the hot-house atmosphere that existed in a girls' school in those days. I did become a kind of heroine by refusing to disclose who had given me the letters, but if, like me, you were on the way to sainthood it wasn't enough being a popular heroine. I would have much preferred to have been a Child of Mary.

Apart from wanting to become a saint, my other great ambition was to be a judge. I never did anything in half measures. I didn't just want to go to heaven like most people: I wanted to be a saint. Likewise, I didn't just want to be a lawyer: I wanted to be a judge. My father spoke of judges with great awe and respect and I thought, 'This is obviously the top of the legal tree and this is where I must go.' I would first have to become a barrister. However, the Professor of Law, Professor McGilligan, said to me, 'Why would you spend all that money becoming a barrister? Who would give a 21-year-old girl a brief to advise on, when they could give the case to a 45-year-old man like your father?' The question seemed absolutely unanswerable to me then. I now look at it with a slightly different logic, but in those days you expected that to happen and I did what the professor suggested.

Selfishly I'm very glad I did. My idea of myself sitting bewigged in court was only a childish dream. I wouldn't have been a very good barrister because I wouldn't have had the patience and discipline to spend hours looking up precedents. I write quickly and I do everything in a slapdash way, which would be a most appalling and impossible trait for a barrister. Being a judge did appeal to me, though. A judge went into court, the case was decided, the judge went home and that was it. It was all so nice and neat, unlike my father's work. God love him, he was always working. He used to bring a big suitcase of briefs wrapped in pink tape with him on holidays to Bally-bunion. Even sitting out in the garden in summertime he would have a bundle of those long brown envelopes with him. The only luxury he would indulge in was reading the *Irish Times*. That kind of life was not for me. It was a judge or nothing. Wasn't it the luck of God that I didn't go that far and upset myself and other people! As things worked out, I did a

BA in university, then I did a Higher Diploma in Education and became a teacher for eight happy years.

When I say that I didn't have any boyfriends at the age of fifteen it was certainly by accident, not by design. I would have been delighted to have had boyfriends but there weren't many opportunities. I didn't have any older brothers. My brother was eight years younger than me and he was no use at all in providing companions. I suppose I did meet fellows at parties, but we were very late developers in our era. In the early Fifties the whole idea of twelve-year-olds having boyfriends was just unheard of; but at fifteen the latent stirrings were there all right, although they were stirring a bit in vain for me. If you were going to be a saint, you didn't think in terms of a 'sex life', but you did think in terms of a good, warm, honest Christian marriage: I did hope that I would get around to that.

When I was about sixteen the first opportunity came my way. Dun Laoghaire on Saturday afternoons was a great place for parading up and down – like the Italian *passeggiata*. We all used to go to the pictures in Dun Laoghaire on Saturday and look with envy at the people who had fellows – I would always be with my sisters or other girls. However, eventually a boy asked me if I would go to the film *Roman Holiday* with him. I was thrilled. I mentioned casually about eighteen hundred times during the week that I was going to the pictures with him on the Saturday. I felt that at last I had joined the gang. He rang the night before to confirm the date. 'I'll see you inside', he said. Oh, the shame and the disappointment! Even now, all these years later, I'd like to get hold of him and beat his stupid, thick head against the wall.

My mother was terrific at explaining the facts of life to us. She told me that she never had them explained to her, so she was determined that she was going to explain them clearly to us. I had known from a very early age how children were born because we had rabbits in a hutch (yes, finally, after my disappointment over my sister not being a rabbit, we did have rabbits), so there was no great mystery in birth; but I wanted to know how babies were conceived. She told me and I flatly refused to believe it. I thanked her very much and decided that this was absolutely impossible; wasn't it terribly sad that my mother was going mad? She was in bed with flu when I discussed the subject with my father.

'I'm very sorry to tell you, Daddy, that Mummy is going insane', I said.

'Why?' he enquired.

'I could not tell you the things that she said,' I replied tactfully, 'but she has a very peculiar explanation of how children are conceived.' I gave him a broad outline of her description. 'Don't you think we should get her a doctor?' I asked with great concern.

'Ah, no,' he said, 'I think she had a point. I think a lot of that could be right.'

I thought to myself, 'Isn't he a wonderfully loyal man!'

I went to my first dance when I was seventeen. It was a dance given by two girls who were at school with me and it was in the Royal Marine Hotel. I thought I looked so gorgeous going to that dance that I could hardly keep my eyes off myself. I wore a blue dress that my cousin had lent me. She was much smaller than me so I had a big blue velvet band set down the middle of the dress to let it out. I wore diamante earrings which had made sores in my ears when I was 'rehearsing' for the dance, so I had put elastoplast on my ears and painted it blue to match the dress. I must have looked absolutely *horrific* but I thought I looked so beautiful as I left the house. How sorry I felt for my poor tired, sad, dull parents! Here I was entering the Royal Marine, aglow, the world at my feet.

Nobody – not one single person – danced with me that night. That was a black time. There weren't many dark passages in my childhood but that most definitely was one of them. When I came home that night I had visions of the whole population of Dun Laoghaire telling each other that nobody had danced with Maeve all night.

Growing up in the Fifties, we were really naive and very innocent. There were parties, of course, and rock and roll, and occasionally the great excitement of a barbecue down at White Rock; but the most awful thing that ever happened at one of those barbecues was when one of the fellows (who had long hair) fell asleep and some friends and I cut his hair while he slept. That was the most violent thing I did in my youth – and when I think of all the things everybody else did (or said they did!) . . .

My friends were always being taken up the Dublin mountains in cars. The mountains seemed to have an aura of steaming sex hanging over them; I was always dying to have a boyfriend who would take me to the mountains. I'm sure that nothing ever happened up there but I was dreadfully envious. It was really a very innocent and harmless time. With the friends I had at school then – who are my closest friends now – I had endless conversations about boyfriends. There was no aspect of people's lives or loves that we didn't discuss: whether he really liked her, whether he respected her if she allowed him to kiss her, etc. I'm sure that the boys never talked about that kind of thing at all.

If ever I want to think of the really good times I had as a child, I think of Christmas. We always had a lovely Christmas. The anticipation was, of course, the best part.

On one Christmas Eve I suddenly announced to Santa that I would like a doll's house. This nearly drove my poor parents demented, as they had bought me lots of other things including a blackboard and chalk. They were up all night trying to make a doll's house but they failed. I can see my mother saying in exasperation to my father, 'Wouldn't you think that in all those books like *A Thousand Things a Boy Can Do*, making a doll's house would be one of them?' In desperation they just left me the blackboard with a note written on it by Santa saying, 'Dear Maeve, the doll's house was too big for your chimney but it will come next year.' I burst in on them on Christmas morning, thrilled to have a letter from Santa *in his own hand*. I reckoned that this was a very valuable thing to have.

We would usually have four or five people to lunch on Christmas Day. They weren't homeless people but simply people who had nowhere special to go on that day. My mother was a great one for asking these people to lunch. She argued that it wasn't as if we were a divided family who just came home for Christmas. We were together all year round and here were these people who had no family: end of argument. We children liked some of them but others we found trying and we were somewhat impatient with them. But it was always lovely. We had a big well-stocked table, we had paper hats and crackers – and we had far too much to eat.

Then on St Stephen's Day my father would give my mother a few pounds to take us to Leopardstown races and off we went on the bus. He hadn't the slightest interest in racing and didn't know one horse from another; but my mother loved it, especially meeting people. It was a marvellous, marvellous day.

I suppose some would say that I had a pampered and privileged childhood; but I just think that I was extraordinarily lucky to be born into a family about whom I have nothing but good memories, and for whom I have nothing but regrets that it can't still be there. I was lonely sometimes, I suppose – feeling that I would not be successful because I was fat, for example – but that was only outside the house: at home I never felt fat. At home I felt very loved and very special. My sisters, my brother and I have all remained extremely friendly and when we talk and think back on our childhood we do so with laughter and affection and not with any sense of fear or dread. We simply think how lucky we were.

# Clare Boylan

———

Clare Boylan was born in Dublin in 1948. She was originally a journalist with the *Irish Press* and later editor of *Image* magazine but gave up journalism to devote her time fully to writing. Her output so far – a collection of short stories entitled *A Nail on the Head* and two novels *Holy Pictures* and *Last Resorts* – has been well received. Clare Boylan now lives in Co. Wicklow.

M INE WAS a Dublin childhood – a totally urban middle-class childhood. We were kids who played in the lane and went to the pictures and ate chips.

'We' were my two sisters and myself. We were very, very close. I was the youngest and at various stages my elder sister, who was three years my senior, was a 'twin' to me, while at other times she was a 'twin' to my eldest sister. We circled round each other like little moths in motes of dusty light.

The earliest experience I had of closeness with my sister was of stealing 'snoke'. 'Snoke' was glucose powder. I don't know where we got the name, but we would wake up with this incredible longing for 'snoke' and steal down the stairs in the dead of night to get it. We piled up chairs to get to the high shelf in the pantry where the box of 'snoke' was kept; and it might as well have been 'coke' – such was the 'high' we got from thieving it.

We would create stories together. We invented twin heroines called Arly and Garty; they had wonderful adventures, which we drew as we were too young to write. I remember one occasion when the twins quenched a volcano by pouring tons of marshmallows into it. When I was a little older, it seemed natural to start writing out the stories. But my sister preferred to tell thrilling adventure serials in bed – serials which always stopped when the girl was pinned to the railway, or about to be dropped from the top floor of a building. My sister would then say, 'I'm tired now – goodnight!' It nearly led to murder on several occasions.

Being the youngest had a double effect. Firstly, I was tremendously spoiled by my mother, because the other girls had gone to school and I was still at home. I think spoiling is very good; it made me feel secure. Secondly, and less advantageously, as the others grew older, clothes would be handed down to me – but not toys. Although my sisters grew out of their toys in terms of use and age, they became emotionally attached to them – so I never had many toys. I don't complain about this, because I never had any sense of expectation. I used to buy toys for myself. I remember buying a tea-set and a cloth duck with padded wings. The duck was very useful: I unpicked some stitches in one wing and pulled out some stuffing, and I could then stuff the wing with sweets and take them to bed with me.

I don't think that either my mother or my father really saw children as children. My father was a shy, reticent man who was unlikely to get into the hurly-burly of parenthood. He wasn't a disciplinarian; but then he grew up among generations of rather vaporous ladies who were inclined to faint away at the first hint of a rough wind! It must have been terrifying for him to have a whole house full of these delicate creatures – he wasn't quite sure what to do with them. He was quite old-fashioned, in the sense that he could not envisage women having careers. We would all be well-educated, and he would see to it that each of us was kept in one piece until we were handed over to a husband. We were even forbidden to ride bicycles or roller-skate in case we knocked our front teeth out. I don't think my father ever saw us as being independent.

My mother saw us as potential people rather than as cuddly babies. I don't imagine that she was all that keen on babies, but she did like older children. She had endless patience with children's questions, because she saw all that as a process of growth. When visitors came, we were always there at table to hear the conversation; but as I remember, it wasn't a very enlightening experience – the adult conversation of the time was extremely boring!

My mother was a writer for as long as I can remember. She wrote essays and short stories; and she composed a children's book for us, which entertained us greatly. I remember summer evenings when she sat writing in the drawing-room while we played in the front garden. At some stage we were sent to the shop for pineapple bars and sailor's chews, which were promptly devoured by all, including Mother, with great gusto. When I was a little older – about seven – I used to type out her articles with two fingers, as a reward for which I would be taken to the movies.

To encourage creativity in her children, my mother took the unusual step of painting one of the kitchen walls black and providing us with a box of coloured chalks. She felt that, because children cannot scale things down, they should not be made to contain their idea of a person or a flower to a page in a notebook; they should draw something as they see it, lifesize or even larger. So we used to spend our days drawing on the black wall. This had a number of advantages. As far as my mother was concerned, it meant that we were very quiet and she could keep an eye on us. For our part it encouraged self-expression and we were given prizes for the best drawing. We never realised, of course, that my mother gave the prizes exactly in rota.

My mother was in many ways a most unconventional woman. When my father was away on business she would keep us home from school for two or three days at a time, switch off the radio and turn the clocks to the wall. She would write and we children would undertake curious and elaborate, if often useless, pieces of housework, like washing rugs in a tin bath or making toffee on the kitchen table. We had a glorious time. We went to the pictures in the evening and extended the fantasy by always trying to eat whatever the people ate in the pictures.

I realise now that this was my mother's silent protest against the extremely conventional lives that women lived then. She dressed up to go to the shops as other women did; she put on her high heels, pearls and gloves to go down to the shop for a bag of potatoes! She obviously hated all this, so in the privacy of her own house, when there was nobody around to approve or disapprove, she lived as she wished to live. Of course this behaviour wasn't very much approved of in school; but she felt that she could 'educate' us just as well at home on the odd days that we took off school – and indeed she did. But then she would provide us with a very haphazard excuse, like 'Dear Sister Immaculata, I kept Clare at home from school because she ate too much and got sick.' Of course, appalling retribution followed at school! I was dragged up and made an example of – 'the frightful little glutton who ate so much that she got sick and couldn't do her lessons . . . .'

Retribution apart, I enjoyed school. It was, in a way, another excursion into fantasy. I loved the company of all the other girls. I thought that was tremendously exciting. I loved the competitive element of school – not the academic end, but any competitions involving learning poetry off by heart or singing a song. It seemed full of possibilities. Lessons were frightfully dull. I thought then, and I still believe, that school textbooks were monstrously dull and that it is an absolute offence to children to teach them lessons in the way they are taught through textbooks. I think that the teachers are doing much more now than they did then, but the textbooks, especially geography and history books, were simply appalling. But as I sat there through this torrent of dullness, I had a fantasy that an enormous American with a cigar in his mouth would burst in the door, point at me and say, 'That's the child. I want her', and that I would be cast in a starring role in *Pollyanna No. 2* or something. It never happened.

I had, I suppose, a very isolated childhood. I remember at an early stage saying to myself, 'What am I?', because I didn't know what to identify with. We didn't see very many other children and when we did see them, we didn't seem to live as they lived. I particularly envied poor children, who ate bread and jam and ran around the streets and generally seemed to live a much rougher existence than we did. Further, not having brothers, we didn't know much about boys.

However, at the age of four, I became great friends with a boy who was much older than me. He was a bad influence – the sort who would run after little girls with a penknife – but he was my great friend. We went around together and he would give me flowers. But our friendship came to an abrupt and angry end one evening. I came into the kitchen and sang my mother a song composed of every swear-word and piece of gutter language that had ever been imagined – words my friend had taught me and which I liked so much that I had put a tune to them.

'Where did you learn that?' my mother demanded as she stamped out to do murder.

End of relationship!

We didn't see all that much of our relations, either, but I did love visiting them. They were all so different that it was like visiting foreign countries. One aunt had eight children and they were not well off but to me they were exotic because, like the poor children I envied, they ate a lot of bread and jam – fresh bread – and they ran around screaming. Another set of relations were, I suspect, rather rich: they had a pony and the little girl had a wardrobe full of frilly dresses. There was a set of spinster sisters who lived in great misery but they had a tremendous raspberry garden at the back of the house.

One of my grandfathers was very musical and had in fact made a few private recordings when he was quite old. I loved them, and still love listening to them, because there is something very moving about that frail old voice struggling to retain the notes on what is now a crackly record. When Grandpa was dying, we children were sent in turn to sit with him. In general, it was considered a chore to have to do this; but I enjoyed it because he would pull a box of photographs concerning his musical career and performances from under the bed and I found it very exciting to go through these mementos with him. As a child I loved observing people. I loved looking at people in different circumstances and visits to relations were infrequent, but all exciting.

We made up for our isolation by creating our own fantasy world: telling and drawing stories, listening to the wireless and going to the pictures. We were great picture-goers: we went two or three times a week. In a way, we saw this celluloid world as the real world, rather than the world we lived in. I remember especially the film, *Marcelino*, in which a little boy gets bitten on the foot by a scorpion. Adults somehow never think of dividing truth from fantasy for children, and from the time I saw *Marcelino* I lived in constant dread of being bitten by a scorpion. I used to bank all my toy animals along the end of my bed to protect my feet. But on Christmas night there was a tradition that your toys would be taken away from you, because if Santa saw all the good stuff that you had he would pass it on to a more deserving child; I recall that particular Christmas night as a time of great terror, as I lay awake with my unprotected feet at the mercy of scorpions.

A similar terror arose after seeing *San Francisco*, a film which gave me my first view of an earthquake. All one saw was this crack developing and suddenly the earth opened and people were swallowed up. From then on I leaped in terror over cracks in the pavement because I thought they were all going to become the *San Francisco* earthquake. Nobody ever told me otherwise.

The other thing that I remember about the films of the Fifties was the treatment of sex, which was a great preoccupation with all the little girls I knew. You knew absolutely nothing but wondered all the time where babies came from. Sex on the screen in the Fifties meant that a couple retreated into the bedroom, and the screen went dark and shrieks of laughter proceeded therefrom. We wondered what was it that made grown-ups laugh, because they hardly ever did. We were fascinated by that.

But, of course, in those days children were to be seen and not heard; and adults were not very imaginative, I suspect. It never really occurred to them that children were going to grow up; indeed, often it still doesn't dawn on adults that childhood is a rehearsal for adult life and that all the time children are processing information as clues, in order to find out how to be grown-ups. Not only do they tell them nothing; they don't even take the precaution of excluding them from their own conversations, so that all you hear as a child are the tantalising fragments of adult talk – you have no idea what the conversations are all about and you are not encouraged to ask any questions. I have highlighted this predicament in an incident in my first novel *Holy Pictures*.

In this particular passage, Father has died and Mother has gone into a decline. The neighbours, seeking to revive her, come round with the latest piece of scandal, which is a court case, concerning a young Jewish boy, who is sued by a Jewish matron who had involved him in a contract to make her the mother of God. The contract has failed so it's not exactly a spicy conversation, but it's got hints of seasoning and the children are all ears.

Mother got out of bed. She patted down the pillows and blankets in a soothing manner so that evidence of her occupation was removed. She went to the dressing-table and stood over the litter of teacups, brushing out her hair.

'I think', she said, 'that I shall have my hair cut. Mr Webster admired long hair but a bob would be so much less trouble. Imagine' – she turned to her friends with a little smile – 'a woman, who has seen her husband safely to God, encouraging a man to do that.'

'To do what, mother?' Mary's intent voice startled the women. The children had been as quiet as spiders. They had not so much as extended a hand towards the tray of delicious food. They were fascinated by this woman who was to re-enact the birth of Jesus. They knew all about the dull little figure of the Virgin Mary but there had been no mention of a man in the boudoir. There was Joseph, the carpenter, but it had been impressed on them that he was a blithering old fool.

The women had forgotten about them. 'Run along, girls,' Mother said, looking amused. 'You may take the tray and have a little feast.'

'Why Mother?' Nan said.

'Because this is most unsuitable.'

'Why?'

'Because only rude, unmannerly girls question their mother.' She gave them a stern look. She had to put her hand over her mouth to smother her smile.

*Holy Pictures*

When I was about nine, there was a period of financial austerity in the house. I was only dimly aware of this at the time; but I later realised that my father was in fact out of work for this period. It must have been an incredibly difficult time for my parents. I have no idea how they managed – especially how they managed to maintain appearances and keep everything as it had been.

There was a particular incident which made me aware that something was wrong. Every year in the convent school, four little girls were chosen as flower girls for the Corpus Christi procession. To be chosen was considered a tremendous honour. You had to dress up in white and scatter a basket of petals – just the sort of thing that little girls love to do. I was thrilled to be chosen as a flower girl and I wrestled into my First Communion dress, which I had long outgrown, and other bits and pieces. As we were going for a rehearsal, I overheard the head nun remark to our teacher, 'Look at the cut of her. We can't have someone like *that* leading the procession.' Another child took my place; and of course I was heartbroken and ran home screaming hysterically to my mother.

Instead of being sympathetic as I had expected, my mother was quite angry. 'I quite agree', she said. 'Why can't you dress up decently? There are plenty of clothes.' I was quite puzzled by this, as I knew there were not plenty of clothes. Why should my mother be so angry? Of course it was because my humiliation reflected on *her*.

That was the first time that I became aware that we were short of money. As I grew older I resented the fact that we had been excluded from this knowledge. I felt that it would have been much better to explain the facts to us and have us all pull together, rather than protect and exclude us. I feel differently now. I realise that my parents were very brave to have hidden their worries from me and I am grateful to them for that because it enabled me to grow up free of financial insecurity. It means that I can do things like leave a very secure job to become a full-time writer – which I did. I always feel that there is more money where the last lot came from and I think that if I had gone through the horror that my parents went through at that time, I certainly wouldn't have that freedom.

There was another possible advantage to the convention of adults not explaining to children. In a curious way, we children had more freedom to work out our own lives when adults took no notice and explained nothing. Nowadays adults make such efforts to understand children that they predefine them. It is almost impossible for an adult to give unprejudiced information to a child. Adults always see children as their own possessions rather than as future citizens of the world; therefore they feel quite at liberty to do whatever they want with them – even with the best will in the world – either to keep them as innocents or to make them grow up too soon. Children are thus the necessary victims of adults – but they are also very good survivors.

On her way out through the scullery she dipped her fingers into a stone jar and rubbed flour over her face to take away the shine. She let herself out by the back door. She meant to slip out into the lane and enter Martindale's by the back so as not to be noticed. It was her first party with boys. She did not want to bother Father, but when she came out into the bright sunlight, feeling strange in her stiff party dress, he was there at the end of the lawn, making a bonfire of some letters.

He scowled at her through the ribbons of smoke. 'Where do you think you're off to?'

'Gladys Martindale asked me to tea.' She held out her dish, still covered with a cloth. 'I've made a cake.'

'There are fellows in there!' he pointed. 'Young swine! I can hear them.'

'Some of the girls have brought their brothers,' she said calmly.

'There is music,' he accused.

'Gladys has been given a present of a gramophone. She has invited us all to hear it.' It was amazing the ease with which she could lie this year. It was like being able to speak a foreign language. It took so little out of her that her father could see straight away that she was telling the truth. He had run out of argument.

'Why have you not brought your sister?' he said wearily.

'She doesn't want to come,' Nan said. 'She's in the drawing-room. She's reading.'

He let her go. She unlatched the back gate. 'Here!' he called out angrily. 'What's the matter with you?'

She turned nonplussed. 'Nothing.'

'Look at you. You're like a ghost.'

'I'm fine.'

'Don't argue with me, you're . . .' he could not put his finger on it: the bleached face; the woman's figure defying the confines of the pretty little dress; her listless insolence. He had never expected her to grow up. It offended him. He liked her small and robust. 'You're peaky!'

'I'll be all right,' she promised.

'No, no.' He shook his head sadly. It was up to him. He could not trust anyone else. 'I shall get your mother to boil you a sheep's head.'

*Holy Pictures*

Somebody suggested that I was very like Nan's sister, Mary, in *Holy Pictures*: a conniving and resourceful little fiend! Certainly I think that being the product of a very conventional father and an unconventional mother made me resourceful. Children find their own light; they find what they want. I wanted adventure. I found it initially through my excursions into fantasy at an early age and later by devising my own projects – anything from sales of work to literary or debating competitions – and ultimately, at the age of fourteen, by organising my reluctant sisters into a pop group called 'The Girl Friends'. It was partly boredom, but mostly the desperate need for money that drove me into this latter enterprise. As well as being a member of the group, I was also the business manager. Initially we earned ten shillings a week, playing the Apollo Variety Theatre or the Plaza Theatre on Saturday nights. Later when we became extremely 'famous', the fee went up to thirty shillings, which meant that I had ten shillings pocket money a week – and from then life just got better and better.

I developed an ear for language through my nasty habit of eavesdropping on grown-ups and some of the things I heard then I can still recall, even though I didn't understand them at all at the time. I remember at a very young age eavesdropping on two ladies, one of them well-dressed and the other one slightly disadvantaged and surrounded by straggling kids. I don't know what the subject of conversation was, but it occurs to me that the well-groomed one was advising the under-privileged woman that she ought to take better care of herself, or else her husband would lose interest in her. The poor lady shrieked with laughter and said, 'Ah, sure, he thinks I'm Scheherazade in a knickers and vest!'

The books of my childhood were a strange collection. We had hardly any children's books, and the adult books seemed mostly to be concerned with madness. I remember Antonia White's *Beyond the Glass* and other authors such as Aldous Huxley, Evelyn Waugh and Graham Greene. I was a conventional child in the matter of reading. I fiercely envied a child in school who had the complete collection of 'Noddy' books, but because Huxley, Waugh and others were on the shelves at home, that was what we read. I didn't understand them at all. I thought that it was all dreadful stuff, but now I think that it had quite a considerable influence on me, particularly the writings of Evelyn Waugh. His habit of slightly caricaturing characters to make them a little larger than life to emphasise not the person but the situation; his underplaying of emotions to highlight a situation which is essentially emotional – he did this so well, avoiding melodrama and yet making difficult situations more acceptable to the reader. Not that I'm claiming to be an Evelyn Waugh – but I suppose that *Holy Pictures* has a lot of caricature in it.

That's partly because children see all adults as being mad. Certainly to us as children, the grown-ups we knew – the priests and nuns, people in shops, visitors to our house – all seemed dessicated and ancient and quite eccentric.

'Have you got any loose hair?' she said to Mrs Guilfoyle. She had been waiting a long time. This neighbour wore a dressing-gown in the house but put on a carnation-pink worsted dress when someone came to the door.

Mrs Guilfoyle chuckled. It made her bust wobble. 'You bold little business, you,' she said. 'Your mother'd have your guts for garters.'

'I'm collecting loose hair: women's,' Mary began again.

It threw Mrs Guilfoyle into a frenzy. She laughed until her teeth clicked. She backed off into the hall. 'Mam-zelle dee Ravelais!' she shrilled. She winked at Mary. 'I have a new woman in my top room. Oh, God, she's gas.' She made a mouth like a shovel and whispered as if it was something rude: 'Foreign.'

There was a clatter on the stairs. A thin woman in a greenish black robe fled along the steps in a sideways motion, like an animal. She had a beige, alarmed face. Her black hair was pinned up with a comb. 'You call, Mrs Guil . . .'

Mrs Guilfoyle could not contain herself. She swelled like a paper bag that has been blown up and is about to be banged by a boy to make a noise. 'Mademoiselle de Ravelais,' she snorted. 'This is the daughter of my friend Mrs Cantwell. She wonders if you can help her. She is collecting the hair of loose women.'

Mary held out her pillowcase for the lodger to see.

The woman's hands rose to clamp the edges of her foaming black head. 'I will have no part in this,' she said. 'It is very bad luck. I am saving my hair for my fiancé.'

Mrs Guilfoyle watched her with amusement. 'Bad luck, do you say?' she jeered. 'Well, maybe I can assist after all. Hold your horses, Mary child.' She stamped back into the house.

Mary and Mlle de Ravelais were left to regard each other with suspicion.

When Mrs Guilfoyle returned she had something like a silver coin clutched in her fist. Mary's heart beat painfully, for it looked like a two-shilling piece.

It was a locket, not even pure silver, going syrupy around the edges. Mrs Guilfoyle prised the catch with a red fingernail. 'The lord and master,' she said, with the same look of a paper bag blown up to burst. 'Bad luck,' she muttered. 'I'll give you bad luck.' Her nail made contact and sliced into the opening and Mary could see a man's terrified face, tobacco coloured, peering out beyond the scarlet scythe. The face was now fully seen – or at least as much as could be inspected behind a bristling clump of real hair. It was red hair. It clung to the man's face like a military moustache as if it had been placed there to give him courage.

Mrs Guilfoyle snatched it roughly from the photograph, removing as she did so some of the man's features, his nose and upper lip, for the hair had been glued on. She held up the sparse tuft of virility. 'My husband left me this a memento when he went to fight the wars,' she said. 'This and nothing more!' She dropped the lock into Mary's pillowcase. 'Use that for your bad luck, dear. See if you can make him squirm, the oul' scald. Pity I have nothing more personal.' She winked at Mlle de Ravelais who looked mortified. 'It's all right Mam-zelle dee,' she said with another terrible wink. 'I won't say another word – not another syllable. *Pas devant l'enfant.*'

*Holy Pictures*

My first loss of innocence came with my First Communion. Up to then I had been totally innocent – things like my bad language song, I think, are a great demonstration of that innocence; then suddenly we were told to examine our consciences for sin – and everywhere you looked, there was sin. It was like swarms of rats. Had you eaten something before going to communion? Had you told a lie? Were you jealous of your friends? Had you been disobedient to your parents? You were rotten with sin the minute you thought about it.

Initially, this was quite pleasing, because up to that time you had been such an unimportant and insignificant little wretch in terms of the world that to be a sinner was rather a status symbol, and it gave you a sense of substance. Then you made your first confession and your sin was taken away. Next came communion, when you got dressed up, like a bride, in tremendous acres of tulle and seed pearls and artificial flowers; but you got your sin back because the first thing you felt was *pride*. Then, if your best friend had more stiff slips under her dress than you, you had *covetousness*. You probably had *lust*, too, because you were told about it – the teachers mentioned it and then said that it was none of your business but they knew nothing anyway – so you quite likely had it, whatever it was. Certainly you had *gluttony* on your First Communion day, with all the parties; then there was the money that you collected and the sense of greed that came with it. I remember somebody asking me at the end of my First Communion day, 'How did it go – how was the day?' I said that I made seven shillings and sixpence – and that was the end of my innocence.

Childhood ended when my sister, the one with whom I was

occasionally twinned, began to date seriously a boyfriend, who later became her husband. I was about fourteen and up to then we had always seen men as a sort of festivity. They were like Christmas. They were exciting and attractive to have around, but they didn't seem to have any individual purpose. We tended to giggle at them. Suddenly my sister wasn't giggling any more and I became a nuisance; she wanted to be alone with her boyfriend and kept telling me to clear off. I was absolutely heartbroken, but naturally in another year or two I was feeling the same way. At that point childhood had ended for me.

Looking back from the point I'm at now I think that I had a wonderful childhood and the best possible advantages, because my parents did two things for me: they gave me a sense of my own importance and they let me know that I was loved. I think that a lot of parents don't want to give children a sense of their own importance in case it becomes over-inflated; but we were always told that we were absolutely marvellous and that if anybody said otherwise they were wrong. That gives you tremendous confidence – and it lasts. If your parents have given you those two things – the sense of self and the love – you have them all your life. If not, you're forever looking for them and I don't think that they can be replaced if they're not given by parents. I don't think that anything else matters. I know that at a younger age there were times when I said 'Why did my parents do this? Why didn't they tell me this?' but that all seems so insignificant now. I really do believe that I owe my parents everything.

# Polly Devlin

———

Polly Devlin was born in Ardboe on the shores of
Lough Neagh, Co. Tyrone, in 1944. That landscape
and the childhood she spent in it have provided
Polly Devlin with material for two books: *All of Us
There* – a highly evocative account of growing up in
Northern Ireland in the Fifties – and *The Far Side
of the Lough: Stories from an Irish Childhood*.
Polly Devlin now lives in London and in Somerset.

M Y EARLIEST memory is very much connected with harvest-time on our small mixed farm. I remember jumping off a hay-lifter and when I looked down at my sister who had jumped before me I saw blood pouring from her head. This memory crystallises around the extraordinarily violent image of blood pouring; the sudden eruption of the wound in the middle of the gentle and tranquil landscape. I assume that my sister was taken to hospital.

This incident is deeply lodged in my memory. I must have been about four then. But some twenty years later when I spoke about it to that sister, she said, 'It was *you* who had the wounded head. It happened to *you*!' That seemed a metaphor for the way in which I have viewed childhood; and it also revealed the way in which my sisters and myself were so inextricably linked that even though the accident happened to *me*, I pushed it on to someone else. So my earliest childhood memory of the tranquillity of the countryside mixed with the sudden way that life could turn on you – is at once ambiguous.

The landscape that I grew up in was both ordinary and quite extraordinary. It had two very striking features. On one side was a vast expanse of water, 25 miles long by 10 miles wide: Lough Neagh. And when you turned your back on this great silvery plain there was another plain: an aerodrome which had been blitzed into an intimate landscape of trees and bushes. (Co. Tyrone is often referred to as 'Tyrone among the bushes'; and never more so than in Ardboe, my native place.) We lived in the little peninsula between the two places, with one tiny road leading out to the nearest small village and then on to the bigger town of Cookstown. The farms were very small and it was a poor district, but very beautiful. Very few families lived in this rural area and while the rest of the century moved on, we stayed in this very flat, hidden byplace, a place bypassed by almost everything else.

When fleece is cut from the sheep and collected at nightfall, the fleeces are still live and warm. If the summer night is cold after a hot day, a mist like the haze on the lough clouds the wool and the cooling fleeces stir slightly all night through. In an old wool-room you could hear the fleeces stirring – a faint sound like soft breathing. Our generation in Ardboe were like fleeces cut from the last of the flock.

*All of Us There*

That image comes from Dorothy Hartley writing about England. I read that many years ago and it always stuck with me because although there were no sheep in Ardboe, the notion of the fleece being alive, even though no longer part of the living creature, seems an apt metaphor for my family, who were so deeply connected with Lough Neagh and yet were poised to take the jump to somewhere else. If you hear an old woman talking about horse-drawn vehicles, about hay being drawn in by big old mares, as a picture of pre-1914 life it doesn't cause you any surprise; but such a life was taking place in Ardboe in the late 1940s and early 1950s. We were effectively lodged in an Edwardian time-warp. My father did have a car (my mother was a school teacher and needed a car) but that was I think, except for the parish priest's car, the only car in the district for a very long time.

Lough Neagh played such an enormous role in our childhood that we never analysed it. It was like our parents, being there all the time. It dominated the whole landscape. Wherever you went you could hear the sough and hiss of the lough – without hearing it, as it were. If it stopped then the world would have come to an end. You only really heard it when you had been away for a while and had come back to realise how loud it was.

We have risen in the unaccustomed half-light of the dawn and crept down the stairs and out through the front door into a world that looks astonishingly different because we are the first to inhabit it. We break the seal on the dew and move silently down the road which lies timid in its untrodden light. The wild roses are pale against the dark green of the hedges. The graveyard is shadow and mystery, its denseness pricked by the gleam of the pale trumpets of woodbine that weave and twine about the hedges. The silence is immense.

Any stranger would surely notice the slap and sough and hiss of the lough, but for us that sound is not noise but part of the quietness. The faintest trace of a spume of mist clings to the rushes, and on a fair morning the thorn-trees creak, the lapwings call, and the whole shore has an extraordinary anticipatory paleness. Everything is leached of colour. The dark heaviness of the graveyard lies high above; here below, on the shore, the greens, yellows, brackens, browns, are still within the gift of the light that hangs, tantalising, just above the blanched greedy surfaces of rushes, stones and water. You feel you could creep under the arriving colour as though under the fringe of an almost transparent curtain, your back just brushing it so that the air and sky will sway and ripple up to the stratosphere.

*All of Us There*

It was a magical place. The great cross of Ardboe stood on the only piece of high ground, surrounded by a graveyard. That was our playground, where we lay on the tombstones and climbed the walls of the old ruined abbey, keeping an eye out for King, the water bailiff. At that time the fishing rights were owned by a London firm, so all the local fishermen were classified as poachers. If the water bailiff was spotted, a bonfire was lit on the lough shore and the boats turned for home. It was exciting and hair-raising to watch King in his huge motor-boat come racing towards the small boats. If he caught them it was disaster because he confiscated their lines and fined them heavily. For people who were struggling to make a living it was a nightmarish existence.

Eels were the chief crop of the lough. Every day during the season eels were caught and kept in tanks which were just slightly submerged below the water. We would lie, fascinated, looking down at those extraordinary pewter lengths combing in and out of themselves. We learned to skin eels when we were quite young, also to gut and clean them – something which invariably brought a shudder from people who didn't come from the lough shore. There is a prejudice against eels but in fact they are a great delicacy.

We learned to swim in the lough. The water was always cold and being fresh water it was not at all buoyant, so you had to work quite hard to swim. We were in and out of the boats all the time but we didn't get out on the lough in boats often, because we would be in the way of working men and also because of a superstition that the lough claimed one victim every year. I suppose the fishermen didn't want to be tempting the lough with nice fresh young bait like us, but the days when you did get out on the lough were astonishing. As you went further out and watched the landscape recede from view, the lough became the world.

It was a unique way to grow up, living between those two great flat spaces of aerodrome and lough. Caught between them we were moulded and shaped into something, I think, which was entirely different than if we had grown up in any other part of Europe.

There are seven children – six sisters and a brother. Our births span twelve years yet we seem always to be seven, forged into each other like crystals on quartz, connected by our name, roots, place, our history, as well as by the knotted, clotted tie of blood. Perhaps most obvious of all, we are connected by our distinctive and characteristic family looks.

*All of Us There*

Our lives were so much enmeshed in each other, so netted together, that there was, it seemed to me, no way to extricate myself. The whole metaphor of enmeshment and of nets has to do with the lough, of course, but for each of us it was a great struggle to get free of our sisters because we were so close. We all loved each other but it was also easy to be passionately angry with our sisters, even to loathe them. When you have sisters, the sister has done what you want to do, she has already been where you hope to go. For each of us, therefore, except for the oldest who had the difficult job of being the pioneer, there was always a sister ahead who appeared to be more glamorous, more clever, more successful or who appeared to have more love from our parents. It happens in every family, I suppose, but it was heightened in our case because there were so many of us with only a twelve-year span among us. We sisters all had the same pursuits, we all read the same books, we all did the same things.

The arrival of a brother in our midst was traumatic in a way. He became a focal point for all of us. We admired him and loved him; and we derived a lot of our feelings and stance about men from observing his behaviour. It had been absolutely bred into us that man was superior to woman and suddenly this male arrived in our midst – somebody who was on the same level of living as we were, but who was masculine and therefore on a higher level in another sense.

Everyone suddenly discusses whether or not the weather will hold until the harvest is finished. What makes them uneasy is that the martins and swallows are beginning to fly low over the ground – a sign of impending rain. It seems hard to believe, in this golden haze. One of the men suddenly, to his own and everyone else's surprise, quotes a line of poetry:

> Lo, low over the fields, the swallow wings.

He looks abashed at this rush of blood to the head and another man staring slyly at my father says, 'I don't care if they're walking it, I'm leaving at six.' Everyone laughs but is somewhat shocked, for when the weather is fine they work till it is dark whatever the hour. Our father, lying with his dark head propped in his hand, finishes the verse:

> The cricket too, how sharp it sings,
> Puss on the hearth with velvet paws
> Sits purring o'er her whiskered jaws.

There is a silence, and a collective gesture towards some vanished schoolroom, and the shadows lengthen at the far edges of the aerodrome.

The blue dome darkens. Ellen gathers up the plates and cups and packs them into the basket. She shakes out the tablecloth and the men put out their cigarettes, some carefully pinching them at the ends and putting them behind their ears to finish later, others grinding them into the stubble. They rise slowly, heavily, and go back to their idle machines. The tractors crash into life, the fanbelts begin to spin, the grain pours through wooden spouts into jute bags attached below them which grow as fat as Nellie's rump within minutes. We thrust our hands into the golden spill and turn them round and round as though washing them in a golden downpour, as if summer could solidify its liquid essence as winter can in snow and hail.

Our father examines the grain, running his hands through it in a different manner, rubbing individual grains between his fingers. He rarely works in the fields – only when one of the men is away or is taken ill – and this is a rare occurrence. He always wears a suit and sometimes a large black leather coat and trilby hat, and when he is lying down on the stubble, languid but full of a tensile energy, he looks to me like the young Elizabethan gallant in the Isaac Oliver reproduction in one of the encyclopaedias at home, although that young beauty is dressed in elaborate and embroidered costume.

*All of Us There*

I don't think that portrait of my father could be that of an ordinary man. My father is an extraordinary man, a man who inspires affection. As a child, I loved him passionately. Every passage in *All of Us There* about my father is obviously a central axis from which I spin. I make him appear so serious in that book. I don't exactly know why, because he is a funny man, full of anecdotes and ways of making people laugh. He has the great gift of reassurance. He had time for you as a child. I find it quite difficult in my own adult life to make time for my own children; I tend to hurry them. But my father never hurried me. He was exceptional for this time because life was not easy then. Money was scarce and as a child you fended for yourself. You kept out of harm's way. To be 'good' was a matter of keeping your head down and not being 'a notice box', as we would say. Being 'a notice box' was simply asserting your ego. If a child does that today, it's taken as a healthy sign, but in my childhood if you asserted your ego you were taken to be a 'cheeky wee girl'. I realise *now* that those 'cheeky' children were in fact very courageous children who stood up for themselves, particularly at school where the rule was to keep your nose clean and your powder dry.

It was quite a cruel dispensation in which children were brought up. So many parents are hoping for something from their children or pushing them or being disappointed in them, but our parents were so manifestly proud and admiring of us and that, I think, is very rare if not unique.

Although she bore seven children within ten years, my mother only stopped teaching for a short time before and after each of our births. Soon after Elizabeth was born, Ellen came to work for her in the house and remained with us until we had all left home. Ellen always seemed to me to be ageless, fixed in a time of her own, infinitely powerful and adult, but I realised as I grew older that she must have been a very young girl, only fifteen or sixteen when she first came to live with us. She was fixed in our early lives at the centre of the domestic life of the house, and she cooked and cleaned and looked after us with the household – and there were usually three children under five years of age at any one time.

*All of Us There*

Ellen was an extraordinary person. She had a sly and ironic way of looking at the world that we, as children, relished. We feared her as we feared any adult but we loved her too. She wasn't a surrogate mother, but she was a central figure in our lives. She was a provider of food, as it were; she did all the cooking. In that way – while both working for my parents and being the centre of our lives – she took a stance that was ironic and reassuring at the same time.

She is full of saws. If a piece of food falls on the floor she remarks as she lifts it, 'Clean meat never fattened a pig': or wiping something with her flower-sprigged overall, 'What the eye doesn't see, the heart doesn't grieve after'; or if we ask for a larger helping of food than we eat, she says with satisfied rancour, 'Your eyes are bigger'n your gut'. Anyone who asks for more is called a 'gorb'. If we complain about a smell in the kitchen she is triumphant: 'A black dog smells its own dirt first' – which preempts further discussion; and any even faintly ambitious talk or desire is 'hairy talk for baldy people'.

*All of Us There*

Ellen had the most amazing turn of expression of anyone I ever met. She had quips and saws and proverbs, and she had a ready saying for almost any occasion. I got my first love of the local way of speaking by listening to Ellen. She let nothing pass without comment. She would call a woman of her own age a 'blade' which is of course a word for a young dandy. 'Look at that blade' meant that the woman in question was acting above herself or was too smartly dressed. One of her worst words was 'tackle'. If you were a tackle, you were in trouble: it meant that you hadn't dressed properly or were behaving in a way that didn't reach her standards. She was a stickler for standards, but they were fairly arbitrary standards and as a result she dealt out a rough justice.

Ellen had a fund of stories: not stories that were a part of an oral tradition that had been handed on for centuries, but simple stories, of incidents that had happened to her or to her parents. It was she who told the story of 'The China Doll' which for me became the seminal story of my childhood. It has since been an important part of my emotional baggage, because it was the first delivered knowledge that innocence was no protection for anyone. It was something that had to be lost and when you lost it you had to retain yourself.

Ellen was one of about ten children and she received a china doll from an aunt in America. It was the first toy she had ever been given. She brought it out to show to all the neighbours and the first person she met was a man who was cutting a hedge. 'I got a doll from America, I got a doll from America.'

'Show us the doll', said the man. She gave him the doll, which he put on top of the steps, then took his shears and cut the doll's head off . . .

When I heard that story for the first time (I would have been about six) I thought my heart would break for Ellen.

'What did you *do*, Ellen?' we asked.

'What would I do?' she replied in a very matter-of-fact way. 'I lifted the doll and I went home.'

Some years ago I asked Ellen to tell the story to my own children. She told them the story, laughing, and I heard the same passion, grief and incredulity in their voices as she said in exactly the same matter-of-fact way, 'What would I do? I took the doll's head home.' Did she accommodate the cruelty? That story was my first intimation about innocence; and in every bit of writing I have done since there has been something about the loss of innocence in a cruel way.

Those hours of happiness when, content in each other's company, we found endless diversion, when we jumped dangerously across deep chasms that lay between the teetering stacked bales of straw, when we climbed from beam to beam to look out of the ventilation holes to see the land slipping into the lough, when we played hide-and-seek among the corn stacks, when we lay watching the farm cats suckle kittens in the nests they made in high corners of hay out of reach of dogs and foxes, and when we too made nests in the piled-up hay, thirty feet above ground, sinking into its yielding prickly crispness, so dry it almost burned.

I discover happiness within the curved confines of that high, pink, corrugated-iron building where, through those round holes cut high to each side, just below the sweep of the arched roof, pours a fall of sun so thick and golden, cascading so heavily and continuously through the stoor and dust that where it is trapped by the hay we almost expect an accumulation, a pond of sun, leaking and seeping away into the stiff yellow hay that lay like Rumplestiltskin's gold around us.

*All of Us There*

My sister Marie says that what she unequivocally loved about childhood was its physical and sensual quality. The beauty of our childhood was undeniable. It was so tranquil and a good deal of the time it was golden. There was the endless sound pattern and routine of a small farm: the slow mooing of the cows on their way to the pasture and on their return in the evening; the jangle and jingle of a horse's leathers and reins and the clip-clop of hooves on the roads; the great rumble of the hay-lifter. All of those sounds have disappeared from the countryside. The other noises that I grieve for are the sounds of the corncrake and the cuckoo and the droning noise of machinery at harvest-time. Flax has disappeared too. I remember the mysterious look that the countryside had when the flax was growing – that extraordinary blueness. I loved too that acrid smell of rotting flax. It was in a way like silage, but silage has a kind of plastic smell to it that I dislike and slurry I find offensive; but I loved the smell of flax – that rich, noisome smell. Those smells, those sounds, are part of a way of life that has totally vanished.

It is curious that I only discover that childhood happiness when I am writing. My child's view of that hay shed, indeed of childhood, seemed that of a dark place – a place where I could have made something *more* of myself. But when as an adult I ventured back rather fearfully into my memory in search of what had happened to me and of the reasons for what I had become, I discovered that neither the hay shed nor the past were so dark. Life had been full of glory and full of sun, yet in my memory I had made my childhood very unhappy. There were of course elements in it that were uniquely happy – like my parents always being there and the place being very beautiful – but none of that helps a child to come to terms with whatever grief she is harbouring. Why had I felt such pain? That was in fact why I started to write *All of Us There*. I couldn't *not* write that book. There was a sort of boulder in my adult path which was childhood. So I ventured back in my writing and discovered that the sun *had* shone, that life had had glorious moments. It was a revelation, finding that I didn't need to make childhood unhappy, that it was no longer necessary to say 'I am full of pain'. I think a lot of children do appear to be quite happy while nourishing pain and resentment internally and they never wholly come to terms with that. I felt that I couldn't go on *not* coming to terms with my interior grief and I suppose the bonus of writing the book was finding how happy I had really been and how much loved I was in that childhood.

As a social system our Catholic religion constituted a tyranny – not within the confines of our family but certainly outside it. We as a family were brought up in a dispensation that was different from that heavily mediaeval Catholic one that obtained in the parish. My mother was brought up in War-renpoint, Co. Down, and even the geographical jump to Co. Tyrone had made her outlook different. My father had been brought up in an enlightened way so that not only was there no bigotry in our house, there was a real tolerance. The parish, however, was run as a great many Irish parishes were run at that time, by priests who brooked no opposition of any kind. The men were mixed with the office to an intolerable degree, so that if you had any quarrel with the man, as it were, you then had a quarrel with the whole church. Quite often at church on Sunday priests would denounce from the altar things that they had no business denouncing: secular affairs, the parishioners' own private business. There were of course good priests and there were bad priests; there were priests who did their best and priests who did their worst. For me, it constituted a tyranny, because there was no escape, no court of appeal. They were the people to whom you confessed but they were also the people who judged you. There was no other tribunal.

That tyranny also extended to school. I wasn't happy at either of the two schools I attended under the care of nuns. I had no quarrel with the nuns as persons – they were women doing their job of work and dedicating themselves to God – but I do find the whole concept of nuns a most mysterious one. I felt then that we were often punished for existing because *their* children did not exist. A great argument for nuns is that they lavish more time and affection on you because they don't have children of their own; but it seems to me that if you have no children of your own you are ill-equipped to give advice about someone else's. It was difficult enough for us as adolescents, being part of a disadvantaged Catholic minority, but in the school I attended you were not encouraged to seek out who you were. You were actively encouraged to seek modesty and humility as the only paths towards some future reward. I'm not that interested in future rewards if it means that sort of abnegation at a time when you need to be given an idea of yourself. My already very tentative idea of myself was much eroded by the women in whose charge I found myself, by women who were supposed to be my mentors and who were full of a self-loathing that certainly boded no good for their charges. I left school a damaged person, bruised and ill-educated. I have a deep abiding bitterness and resentment about my 'education'.

Books were my escape and my path into the future – along with the good luck of having my sisters and my parents. My sisters are women of such quality that even talking to them would always give you a new stance and a new outlook on life; but books were a completely new avenue to the future. I had two sources of books. Above my father's pub – an Edwardian building – there was a loft into which had been put the books that had been jettisoned from the main house. These were books that my mother might have censored or books that people had got tired of – things like *Ripley's Believe It or Not* and a vast store of Victoriana – books on etiquette and household matters. Lying up in that loft, you could hear the murmur of the men's voices below us as they drank their Guinness; and the local dogs would come up to the loft because it was warm. We would lie up there, reading authors like Mrs Humphrey Ward , caught in our time-warp.

The other source of books was, as it were, archives from the future. These were year-books which were sent to my mother by her half-sister, who was headmistress of a private school run by the Marymount nuns outside Los Angeles. I had never seen anything like those books. They were great big, fat, glossy things, bound with a kind of vinyl material – it was like a growing material, like a mushroom in my hand. When I opened each book there was a 'year' of the school spread out for me. There were photographs of girls with make-up and blonde hair, girls dancing, skiing, film-making, riding, making music – activities that were *light* years away from what *we* were doing; but what was so extraordinary was that those girls were being educated by *nuns*. They were 'good Catholic girls' and yet they were leading a life that seemed to me to be open, sunny, glorious, free and full of ego-boosting activities. I couldn't reconcile my dark, dark, miserable 'Tom Brown' schooldays with those glorious sunny schooldays in Los Angeles. Maybe if I went back properly into my schooldays I might find that there was happiness, as there was in the hay shed, but those year-books were certainly a leap for me into the future. They gave me the determination to leave my darkness behind and to get into an inch of space that was sunny for myself.

> All children born in segregated places are born with a dark caul, a web of ambiguities around them, from which it is difficult to struggle free. But the Roman Catholic children of the province of Northern Ireland have a darker, stronger birth-membrane imprisoning them against which they have to struggle, since the loyalties and love we feel towards our putative nation and power-ful religion are subversive. Loyalty towards the idea of Ireland and love for Mother Church are inextricably entangled, yet neither feeling can be open, proud or free, since neither religion nor country has status, official sanction or respect.

*All of Us There*

Growing up in Northern Ireland puts you in a most am-biguous position. You are Irish and you are officially British; you live in Ireland and yet it is part of the United Kingdom. I knew every date of every English king but I knew nothing about Irish history at all, except in a vague peripheral manner, where it touched on English history. The government was almost wholly Protestant. There were few representatives of your own religion and of your way of life and yet you were governed by people who purported to represent you. In a way you were non-existent. There was a kind of uneasy truce going on when we were growing up – this was long before the present troubles – but that truce had a great deal to do with the Catholics being what *we* were taught to be at school – 'Be good and don't be "notice boxes".' That was why that society was able to jog along as it did: because we kept quiet, kept our heads down. I think elections and things like that have changed things for the general good. God knows, what is happening is nightmarish, but I think it's preferable to being cowed into silence and submission and not having any way out at all, which was our situation. As long as you kept your head below the horizon you could get by, but you had no power. You had no sense of yourself. You were of an inferior race and if you added *that* to the problems of being a woman in a male-dominated society, you really had your problems.

# Jennifer Johnston

———————

Jennifer Johnston was born in Dublin in 1930, the daughter of Denis Johnston, novelist, playwright and war correspondent, and Shelah Richards, a noted actress and theatre director. She has written a number of plays but since 1972 she has produced a succession of highly-acclaimed novels – *The Captains and the Kings*, *The Gates*, *How Many Miles to Babylon?*, *Shadows on Our Skin*, *The Old Jest* and *The Railway-Station Man*. Jennifer Johnston now lives in Derry.

MINE WAS very much a Dublin childhood. I was born, reared and schooled in the city, although curiously the very earliest fragment of memory that I can recall is of sitting on my grandfather's knee in Greystones, Co. Wicklow. He was very old and was wearing a panama hat. It is a fleeting memory – like an old photograph – and since my grandfather died when I was about two and a half, I must have been very young indeed in the scene that I recall.

For the first few years of my life we lived in a flat in Fitzwilliam Square in Dublin, so my memories of that time are of walks in St Stephen's Green and feeding the ducks there. We also played in the little park in Fitzwilliam Square – I remember a swing there with affection. Shortly before the war we moved out to an old Victorian house in Stillorgan. My godfather lived in the bottom half of the house and my mother, my brother Michael and myself lived in the top half, where there were lovely big rooms and lots of light – and where it was very cold in winter, as I remember.

My parents were Denis Johnston and Shelah Richards, who were noted figures in the literary and theatrical worlds, but of course I wasn't conscious of their fame as a small child. To me they were just Mother and Father and the life I led seemed to be the norm. I had a good relationship with my parents. I was quite protected; or rather they were well protected from me and my brother, Michael, by Nono, a nanny who looked after all our wants and wishes and kept us safe from our parents and our parents safe from us. Consequently, our parents only saw us when they wanted to, which worked out quite well because they were then in a good and receptive mood. We also had a

marvellous housekeeper called May. Nono and May were
from totally different backgrounds. Nono belonged to some
fringe Protestant religion, possibly Plymouth Brethren. She
was a very upright and good woman. May came from an
ancient Dublin Catholic family. She had brothers, nephews
and nieces who all became very much a part of my life. I
remember going out to Drumcondra to visit an old aunt of
May's, so her family became my extended family – more so
than my own cousins who were much older than me.

The fact that Nono and May came from different religious
traditions didn't enter into my relationship with them at all. In
fact, it reflected my own lineage in part. My mother's middle
sister married a Catholic and all her children were Catholics. If
I stayed with that aunt it was quite a normal thing to go to Mass
with my cousins; whereas if I stayed with my aunt in Greystones I would go to the Protestant church. She wasn't a great
churchgoer but during the war she had a son in the Royal
Marines and every now and then she would announce, 'I have a
feeling Tony needs to be prayed for', and off the pair of us
would troop to pray for my cousin. She was a great lady. I
loved her very much.

I was fairly indifferent to religion as a child. I was attracted
to churches more by atmosphere than by any religious practice. I loved the smell and feel of a Catholic church. I infinitely
preferred that to the antiseptic atmosphere and the emptiness
of the Church of Ireland. When you walked up the aisle of that
church your feet clattered on metal grilles and you felt terribly
alone and confronted with God, whereas the Catholic church
was warm and embracing and I loved that. For many years a
great friend and I used to go into Donnybrook Catholic
Church on our way back from school. If we had any spare
pennies we would light candles and sit there and look at people
and think, 'This is so lovely!' We were sucked into the
atmosphere.

I discovered at the age of twelve that I hadn't been
christened. My parents had decided that they would be terribly
liberal about religion and they would not have either Michael
or myself christened until we were old enough to decide what

religion, if any, we wanted to adopt. I have a very clear memory of the local curate, Mr Hanson, coming to the house one winter's evening and saying to my mother, 'I've just come to talk about Jennifer being confirmed.' My mother burst out laughing and said, 'She hasn't even been christened!' I was appalled at this because it carried a terrible social stigma, apart from the fact that I had within me the awful mythology of Limbo which I had acquired from Catholic friends. I was quite convinced that if between that moment and the moment of being baptised I were to fall off my bike and be run over by a No. 8 tram, I would go straight to Limbo where I would spend a horrible eternity. I wasn't going to take any chances: I stopped going to school on my bicycle for six weeks until the christening actually happened.

Michael and I were duly christened. I never told any of my friends; it was all too embarrassing. The grown-ups thought it was a great idea. We had a great lunch party before the christening and I remember my mother handing around bunches of parsley to everyone to eat. She didn't want the guests to arrive at the church smelling of gin and tonic!

That incident reminds me of an earlier one when I had a glass of champagne. Before we moved to Stillorgan we rented a house in Rathmines in which I had a tiny bedroom at the end of a passage. I used to read in bed with a torch under the bedclothes – something which landed me in terrible trouble because I was told it was bad for my eyes. On this particular night I was caught once again and taken out to the drawing-room, expecting the worst. Instead, I found a party in full swing, celebrating the coronation of King George VI.

It was a bizarre occasion. Instead of being lectured for reading in bed, I was given a glass of champagne. Whether this indicates an Anglo-Irish tradition in our family or not, I can't be sure. I remember that my mother had a little stone bust of Edward VIII; my parents were great admirers of his and they thought the abdication was a terrible tragedy. But as for celebrating the coronation, I think it was a case of any excuse for a party . . .

My godmother was the artist Beatrice Glenavy. She lived in a lovely big yellow Georgian house in the foothills of the Dublin mountains. She would hold *salons* on Sunday evenings and I was brought along on those occasions. I was very shy, and anyway one was not expected as a child to join in the conversations, but I would observe what was going on and listen in. We were all very concentrated on ourselves in this country at the end of the war and it was marvellously exciting to find intelligent people – painters, writers and actors – from outside Ireland coming to this house and talking about the world. Through them I discovered that there was a world outside my world – a world that I was totally unaware of, except in a vague, romantic way.

I went to school at the age of three which was unusually early. I had problems with my eyesight and I was sent to school at that age in order to learn to recognise letters. The school was Park House and I stayed there for fourteen years. It was a small school which was started by a Miss Phail. It began as a preparatory school but when the war came it continued as a secondary school. I was, with nine others, in the first group that proceeded to secondary school. This was unhealthy in a way because we were the top class right through our schooling and so we had nothing to work towards: everybody else was coming up underneath us.

Miss Phail was a most enlightened woman and a very literary person. She was very friendly with the Synges and the Yeatses, so all her classes were permeated with a slightly romantic 'celtic twilight' aura. She introduced us to the great artists and the great composers – I remember her bringing in gramophone records and playing the music of Bach for us. She tried to turn us into liberal thinking people, but when she died the school became more traditional and fell apart at the seams. There seemed to be no time any more for a lot of the good things and as a result I grew very bored and I really hated school from then on.

For some mysterious reason my mother decided that I would become a more acceptable person if I learned dancing, so I was despatched to the Abbey School of Ballet where (the theory was) I would learn to stand up straight, carry myself properly and move graciously – all the things that little girls ought to do. I hated the whole experience because I *knew* that my knees were going to bend in the wrong direction when everyone else would get it right and that I was going to be the one who would be picked out. There was a basic arrogance in me, I suppose; I felt that I would always be the one to be picked out for wrongdoing, even if I was in the right.

I also hated the journey home on my bicycle from the Abbey School of Ballet. In my mind, it seems I was always making this journey on dark winter nights. I used to invent this great journey for myself. I was never riding a bicycle – I was riding a horse or having some exotic adventure – and I was always a boy. This fantastic journey would get me home without really feeling the pain of riding a bicycle.

I suppose that, given the literary environment in which I grew up, it was inevitable that I got caught up in books. I read everything, absolutely everything that I could lay my hands on, and I read all the time – even when I shouldn't have been reading, as when I read under the blankets with a torch. I always walked around with books in my pockets – books that weren't always necessarily suitable reading for me at the time. There was only one book that my mother ever told me *not* to read. I can't remember the title, but it was a book about concentration camps and she was quite adamant about my not reading it. I read everything else though – and that was a lot, because the house was full of books and I used to buy books with my pocket money, just like young people buy records and tapes today. I read all the classic children's books – like *Alice in Wonderland*, which I must have read about forty times. I loved that book particularly because the marvellous feeling of its fantasy world was something that I had going on in my head. I had a very lively imagination and, as with the journey home from ballet school, I told myself a story to get myself through whatever it was I had to do. When my brother Michael was quite small we shared a bedroom and I told him endless stories.

He used to stay awake until I came to bed, when I would tell him long complicated stories about little furry animals and teddy bears.

When I was about nine my parents were divorced. To an outsider this may seem a traumatic experience for a child of that age, but I was unaware that it was happening. My father had been working in London and Belfast and when the war began he became a war correspondent, so he only came home on leave and then he would stay with my grandmother. My parents' separation didn't seem peculiar to me at that stage; because of the pattern my life had taken up to then, I didn't feel a sense of loss. I had not been really involved in actual day-to-day living with my parents. I had led a very protected life and I was therefore protected from the pain that they must have been feeling. It wasn't until very much later that I was aware how terrible a time it must have been for all concerned and that I should have felt much more pain than I actually did.

I suppose the divorce did colour my relationship with my father. I found it quite difficult to communicate with him. I think that when I was in my teens, there was some sort of anger inside me, which I bottled up and therefore I was always quite closed up with him. There was an abnormal distance between us. After the war when I used to stay with him and his wife, Betty, I had a feeling that I shouldn't enjoy myself because I would in some way be letting my mother down.

I wasn't necessarily drawn closer to my mother when the divorce came. I don't think that I felt any great need to protect her in any way, but I did feel that I ought to have a loyalty towards her and therefore should not let her down by displaying great affection towards my father. Consequently I distanced myself from him and he in turn thought I didn't like him, which of course was untrue. We were all constrained by the divorce.

My mother brought us up in a very traditional way – more or less in the way she would have been brought up herself. We had to go to bed at the right time and we had to do what we were told. She didn't like us gallivanting around as teenagers and even when I was in Trinity College, Dublin, I was not allowed to go into a pub. Needless to say I broke that rule regularly but it often happened that when my mother was rehearsing in the Gaiety Theatre and I was in some pub off Grafton Street, somebody would tip me off that my mother was coming. I simply had to drink up my glass of wine or whatever and scamper out of the pub.

My early childhood was very sheltered but also very secure despite my parents' separation. I wasn't really a 'loner' but I was never good in groups. I liked my friends individually but I couldn't take five or six of them together. I always withdrew in a peculiar way. I couldn't bear summers in Greystones because, although I loved my aunt dearly, my cousins were all at least ten years older than me and I was just a nuisance. Everybody played tennis which I couldn't play, so I felt very inadequate and very much on my own.

Almost from the moment I started thinking, I really would have preferred to have been a man. I wouldn't want to be a man now, but it seemed to me as a child that it was a man's world. The world was for men and I couldn't work out where I fitted into it. I certainly didn't see myself taking up the woman's role and in all my dreams and imaginings I was always a boy. It took me quite a long time to work out the fact that you had to take what you were and attack the world from that standpoint. I think that I must have been a very neurotic teenager.

My mother was of course the epitome of the career woman. She did marvellous things on stage, but then my mother was a very extraordinary person and it never occurred to me that I could be an extraordinary person. She wasn't like other people's mothers; nor was she like her own sisters, so therefore she seemed unreal in a way. You just had to be so different to be able to cope with the sort of life that she was leading and I didn't really ever feel that I had that in me at all. Whenever she was rehearsing in the Olympia or the Gaiety I would cycle there after school, creep into the dark auditorium and move around and watch what was happening on-stage. I was totally stagestruck.

I thought that this was really life and living in the way I wanted my life to be, but it didn't work out like that. When I left school at seventeen years of age I did say that I wanted to go on stage but my parents were distinctly unenthusiastic about the idea. At one point my father said to me, in a very patronising way, 'Oh, you just want to be an *actress*,' and I thought there must be something terribly wrong about that. My mother's reaction was, 'Well you can either go to Trinity College or I will see if Hilton (Edwards) will give you a job . . .' I was living at home and I presumed that they both wanted me to go to Trinity College. It wasn't really an either-or situation. I didn't fight my corner at all. I went to Trinity College.

I have no regrets at all now about that decision. I feel that if I had gone into the theatre I wouldn't have done any writing; and I think that I am a much better writer than I would ever have been an actress. I would have liked to direct plays, but at that point in my life directing was a distant dream which would have been totally unattainable. I am very glad that I went to college – and that in itself was not easy. I had never really settled down to work at school and at the age of seventeen I suddenly realised that I did not even have a basic education. I had great difficulty getting into Trinity College and when I did get in, I was terribly disillusioned with what was on offer – just sitting in a class of an enormous size, listening to tiresome old men talking to us about Shakespeare. I had expected to be illuminated by university because I had a vision of all those lovely intelligent people, growing up acquiring knowledge and knowing what to do with it, but university wasn't like that at all. It was a peculiar time in university because it was just after the war and there was a great influx of ex-service men. You couldn't really call them men, God love them. They were senior to the ordinary students, mostly in their early twenties. They were both glamorous and dangerous. They had all been at war and had seen something outside Ireland, which none of the rest of us had done. They seemed terribly sophisticated, but most of the time they were getting drunk and making an awful nuisance of themselves. They were frightening to us, which in a way made us seem very much younger than in fact we were.

We felt like schoolchildren because we had to fight against this great body of 'sophistication'.

I did some writing as a child. I used to write plays which we acted out in school concerts; and I remember that my school essays were full of terrible 'purple' passages. I was never a critical writer. I used to write what is now called 'creative prose', but I stopped writing at the age of seventeen because I was so confused. I felt at a terrible disadvantage because I realised that I hadn't got anything much out of school except a great desire to read. That didn't seem enough to me and when I went to Trinity College to study English, I soon became very disillusioned there.

I was a mess at that stage of my life. I hated being seventeen. I found the world a very daunting, at times terrifying place. In fact, I didn't much like being anything until I was thirty. It took me that long to sort myself out, to work out what my role in life was and where I was going. Perhaps I wasn't exceptional in that. Most of my peers had no great expectations of life at the age of seventeen. They did secretarial courses, or became teachers, and eventually married and had children; but beyond that they never did anything with their lives. They had no expectations that they might do anything at all that was outside the normal course of traditional events.

When I began to write seriously a lot of my writing was set in 'big houses' which I suppose reflects on my childhood to a certain degree. The houses that I wrote about were never really very big. They were just rather crumbly country houses that one's friends lived in, where people had time to sit down and talk to you – old men would talk to you about the First World War, for example. Even though my mother's parents were not immediately 'big house' people, that was their sort of background and there were always undertones of that background in my life and ultimately in my writing.

The first flight of stairs had tarnished brass rods holding the carpet in place. Nellie used, once a week, to slide each one out from its slots and polish it golden and for a while the hall and stairway would smell of Brasso. She sang always as she did this job. Sometimes now as the old man climbed the stairs, her voice came into his head. 'Come back to Erin, mavourneen, mavourneen. Come back, machree, to the land of your birth . . .' The cloth would squeak as she rubbed it up and down the rod and the smell of the polish flew up your nose and made you sneeze if you happened to be passing.

The top flight had only tacks which held the remaining rags of carpet to the floor. Up at the top, the long passage between the locked doors was lit by two half-moon windows, one at each end of the passage, perfectly symmetrical. Long creeper fronds tapped against them now, incessantly, impatiently, wanting in . . . The light in the passage was constant twilight. The smell was musty and all the time the tiny noises made by unused rooms brushed your ears. The end room on the right had been the nursery. Three windows to the south-west caught the afternoon sunlight in tangles of spiders' webs. Everywhere that dust could lie was filmed with grey. The chairs were sheeted. A large grey bear with one eye stared down from the top of a cupboard.

'It was the nursery. The playroom,' he explained, seeing the boy look puzzled. 'Look.' He opened a cupboard. Inside on the dusty shelves, neatly stacked as if only yesterday some creaking, crackling nanny had tidied them away, were boxes of soldiers and equipment. Each box was carefully labelled, spidery thin-nib, black writing, starting to fade now after many years. Black Watch, Lancers, Gurkhas, Field Artillery, Red Cross, Foot Guards, Dragoons, Legionnaires. Miscellaneous. 'My brother and I were great collectors.'

The boy moved to the cupboard and opened one of the boxes. He stared, fascinated, at the soldiers.

'We were very proud of them. Mind you, they're a bit out of date now. It must be almost sixty years.' He nodded to himself and whispered quietly, '. . . or more.'

Diarmid was lining some men up along the edge of a shelf.

'. . . More. A bit more than sixty years since the last ones were bought. He was older than I.'

'What was his name?' He didn't sound really interested. He opened another box.

'Alexander. After my father.' The boy picked out a galloping horseman. 'That's an Uhlan. Ever heard of them?'

'No.'

'A very famous German regiment. There's a book downstairs. It will tell you all about them. We'll have a look later.'

'Thanks. Where is he now?'

'Who?'

'Alexander. He must be very old. Or is he . . .?' He paused discreetly.

'He's gone a long time ago.'

'Gone?'

'1915.'

*The Captains and the Kings*

I was quite a lonely child. I always felt that I was an outsider, even with people that I knew very well. When I looked at my friends they seemed to be able to come to terms with the world much better than I did. They seemed to be able to fit into living in a much easier way than I did. I was always uneasy about this, because I was quite a nice child really.

One of my great crimes was that I wasn't 'sporty' while everyone else was: my mother was quite a good tennis player, all my cousins played tennis and golf, everyone sailed – but I was never really able to do these things. I couldn't see properly and that may be one reason why I was always an outsider. I was always a nuisance in group activities. If we went mountain climbing, everyone else had to wait half an hour for me to get down the mountain. They probably didn't mind at all, but I was always convinced that they were all standing there at the bottom of the mountain saying 'Ah God, why doesn't Jennifer hurry up!' I would arrive in a state of nerves and start apologising. I was quite an apologetic child. I seemed to spend a lot of time apologising for not doing things that I felt I ought to be able to do.

The compensations for the loneliness and unhappiness were, of course, books and the great fascination for the theatre. As I grew into my teens, my friends were quite envious of my having famous parents. That set me apart in a strange way. It seemed that almost everyone in Dublin knew my parents, particularly my mother (my father was abroad most of the time). Often I would cycle home at night without a bicycle lamp and when I met one of the local Gardaí, he would shout across the road at me, 'Haven't got your light again, Jennifer! How's your mother?'

At other times I could be terribly embarrassed by the fact that my parents weren't the same as everyone else's parents. I think that when you are growing up you want to fit into some pattern but you don't see a big enough picture to know what that pattern really is. You just see a very narrow social pattern into which you have been put and if you are spilling out over that in some way it can be very embarrassing for a child.

I suppose my upbringing did influence my attitude to my own children. I did protect them but I also tried to show them the world a little more. They were brought up in London, in a state of total confusion. They tell me now that I was obsessive about their Irishness, to the extent that they were sent to a French school! I used to bring them back to Ireland as much as possible and my warm talking to them was always about Ireland. I had always felt an alien in London and I think that this disconcerted my own children.

I would love childhood to mean a sort of free growing but in reality it never is, because, I think, all children, no matter what their background, have dark corners which they keep to themselves. There is never the openness between children and parents that one would love to see. I don't think that there ever can be that openness – it's just the nature of the beasts, both parents and children. The one cannot actually see life from the perspective of the other, and so the 'dark corners' become caverns of misunderstanding and misinterpretation at times. It's only when you're grown up that you can actually come to terms with those misunderstandings and see your parents as they really are. Similarly, parents looking at children see them as people they love, people they have to protect from the world (probably quite wrongly) and people for whom they have *their* particular expectations. There are of course marvellous moments of great happiness; but there are also inescapable pains and disappointments.

# Molly Keane

---

Molly Keane was born in Co. Kildare in 1904 into 'a lovely country-house life' which was later to become the material for her books. Between 1928 and 1956 she wrote a number of plays and published eleven novels under the pseudonym M. J. Farrell. The sudden death of her husband when he was thirty-six left her to struggle with a young family and extreme loneliness. She eventually turned to writing again, making a spectacular comeback in 1981 with *Good Behaviour* followed closely by *Time After Time*. Both these very successful novels have been adapted for television. Molly Keane now lives in Co. Waterford.

My VERY earliest memory takes me back to when I was about three years old. I was alone, looking through a doorway into the stable yard and on the saddle-room door were nailed my father's hunting breeches. I thought it was my father who was nailed to the door and I became terribly upset. I can't think why, because I didn't know him very well. That was in Co. Kildare where we lived for the first five years of my life, before moving to Co. Wexford where I spent the remainder of my childhood.

That early memory was, I suppose, symbolic of my father's life. Horses were his whole life and he was very much part of the hunting society. He was born in England, the youngest son in a family of twelve. My grandfather must have been pretty rich because he bought an enormous ranch in Canada for my father – but in those days you could buy hundreds and hundreds of acres in Canada for about fourpence an acre. My father went there in about 1860 – it seems about a thousand years ago – and he loved the ranch, which he stocked with cattle and horses. He adored horses and he was a beautiful horseman. We, his children, all had ponies and donkeys when we were very young but we were never taught to ride. We were supposed to inherit the ability . . .

My father was a very remote figure to me as a child. He just didn't enter my life very much and when he did it was a dreadful chore for him. Each Sunday afternoon he used to take us children away in a pony and cart to a place we called 'the wild wood'. He would light a sort of campfire there sometimes, which we loved, and he would read to us from *The*

*Jungle Book* or *Tales of the Blackfoot Indians*. That was the one time in the week when we saw our father but it didn't really draw us any closer to him. It was a task, a duty he had to do. My elder brother got on marvellously with my father. He was terribly good on his pony and a very good shot and so he had much more in common with my father than the rest of us had.

There were five children in our family and I came in the middle of the five. I remember having an awful time with my elder sister. We never got on together as children (we did much later on as adults) and I used to team up with my elder brother against her. Children really are such beastly creatures! We lived in a very isolated country way where one made one's own amusements. One had one's pony or donkey, the hayloft to play in and the companionship of all the people who worked in the house or on the farm. They were our real companions – the adults, not their children – and we simply loved them.

My mother was practically a recluse. She was certainly a social recluse: she wasn't at all interested in the social life about her. For all that, people liked her. She had close friends and she was very much involved in her own family – her sisters, her brother and her cousins. She wrote quite a bit and was rather a good poetess. She did literary reviews for *Blackwoods* magazine, which was then considered to be the very top literary magazine (although to my mind it was mostly full of things that pleased everyone who was far away in India and such places). It was considered an honour to write for *Blackwoods* and they published almost anything my mother chose to write. Her poems were *The Songs of the Glens of Antrim* (my mother came originally from Co. Antrim). They were jolly good poems, too – romantic sort of poems about the peasant life. In those days if you wrote those kind of romantic poems you didn't write them about yourself – you wrote about the poorer class. Even as a writer my mother never mixed in the literary world, which I think would have suited her rather well. She was also very musical but she never really shared her literary and musical interests with us.

I can't really say why, but none the less I was very fond of her. She had a sort of 'star quality' and to me she was a star, even though I didn't see a great deal of her. When I was very young she didn't come into the nursery very much. We would go down to her after tea each evening for about an hour; I would be dressed up in blue velvet and lace frills. She would read aloud to us and then we would be taken back up to bed by half past six. That was the only time of the day when we would actually be with her. One would meet her occasionally out of doors – she was a tremendous gardener and she was very keen on children being interested in their gardens. She was also very religious, and in the mornings we assembled for family prayers – before her breakfast and after ours.

From the age of about six I was in the care of a governess. We had a succession of these, some of whom I liked more than others. One or two naughty ones used to laugh at everything, including my mother, which was rather disloyal, but I suppose children like a rebellious person. I think that the governesses came through some agency in Dublin. Many of them would have been the daughters of badly financed secondary Anglo-Irish families and one or two were English, but we weren't really in their 'care' at all. We saw them for lessons and at meal times but apart from that we were absolutely free. They were in charge of our education, in theory, but we learned nothing from them and as a result I'm probably the worst educated woman in the world! When I started lessons I spent about an hour a day trying to learn to read some positively awful 'cat on the mat' book. Later there were books like Mrs Martin's *History of England*, Gill's *Geography*, some terrible French grammar book whose title escapes me and books of little rhymes and poems, some French and some English – but I learned very little from any of them.

We rose each day at about seven thirty (this was at the age of about nine or ten). We had breakfast in the schoolroom with the governess – usually it was something awful like porridge or fried bread (which was particularly nasty) and milk (which was supposed to be good for you). Mother came in just before 'dining-room breakfast' and read family prayers to us. After that we fed the dogs and from ten o'clock till twelve we had 'lessons'. We were comparatively free for the rest of the day thereafter – except for something awful called 'Preparation' in the evening. Lunch was at about one o'clock. That was the only meal we had in the dining-room but the food wasn't very good and we were at the mercy of the cook. I imagine that the best food was kept for dinner at night, when the cook would also take more trouble with its preparation, but as children we never saw any of that.

The afternoons were long. Mostly you had your pony and you possibly fiddled around your garden, because above all else you were supposed to be out of doors a great deal. (When I was much younger I was out of doors for awfully long periods of time.) There were long hours of wandering about with nothing to do, particularly when my elder brother went to school and the others were much younger than me. I do remember spending hours by myself and being easily frightened by things. At the end of the kitchen garden there was a beautiful place called the Great Nut Walk – a long path among all sorts of nut trees. It was a great place for playing – building houses and things like that – but I remember being terrified there by 'Old Nettle'. He was a dotty old fellow who wandered the countryside and he would often walk up and down the field outside our house. I remember being in the Great Nut Walk and hearing Old Nettle 'booing' like a cow outside. I was terrified and dreaded going to the Nut Walk for a long time after that.

Tea was in the schoolroom – horrid bread, butter and jam – before a very small fire. I don't know why the governess couldn't build up a good fire because, God knows, there was enough wood around the place, but I remember a very large fender and a very small fire – and chilblains always, always awful chilblains right through my childhood. We would go down to the drawing-room after tea (though not as regularly as when we were little) but I don't think we were read aloud to or anything. We just talked. Sometimes we took lanterns and went out into the dark – we rather enjoyed doing that – and then we went to bed between seven and eight. I shared a bedroom with my sister and we hated each other. We also shared the room with cages full of budgies and other birds. We didn't have supper – just biscuits in bed. The place was absolutely running with mice – I suppose between the birdseed and the biscuits they had a royal time!

I went to school at a very late age – I must have been about fourteen. It was called the French School in Bray, Co. Wicklow, probably, I think, because it had been started by some old French lady a thousand years ago. A great-aunt of mine went there so it was pretty ancient.

It was a very odd place. Everybody, girls and teachers – except the English mistress – hated me. I suppose it was because I was a different kind of animal to them, having grown as old as I had in that very isolated way; whereas they had a different upbringing, and had seen much more of the neighbouring children as they grew up. It was a great shock to me, as I had always liked people. I had got on terribly well with all the people who worked at home but now I felt that life would be miserable for the rest of my life.

The school had a very strict régime. There were no 'naughty doings': even the smallest doing was supposed to be dreadfully naughty! You had to make a report each morning on how you had behaved the previous day. Speaking French was the big thing in that school, so the best report was 'I faithfully spoke French and I was punctual.' (You can imagine the awful French we spoke!) The next grade in the report was 'I faithfully *tried to speak* French and I was punctual'; and the worst grade of all was 'I didn't speak any French and I was late.' If you were honest enough to admit that, some ghastly punishment would follow.

Academically I was hopeless. They gave up trying to teach me arithmetic, let alone mathematics! English was taught in a dreadfully bad and dull fashion; and as a result I don't think that I had any understanding of literature until I was at least twenty-five. But despite that I had a certain liking for it, and I loved Tennyson and Kipling especially.

There was another kind of school at an earlier age which I also detested. This was a weekly dancing class which I attended when I was about seven. Some might think that a privilege, but I thought it was absolute torture. It was held every Wednesday in a big house in Co. Kildare (Wexford was really much more savage – there was nothing like a dancing class there!) About twenty-five children arrived each week to take lessons from Mr Leggatt-Byrne (how appropriate the name was!) who came down from Dublin. I remember that he had kid gloves with which he would slap you – and if he wasn't slapping you he was slapping himself in time to the music. I never learned anything at dancing class. I had no ear for music, so it was no wonder! I must have had some sense of rhythm because I got on all right with the dancing later, but then it was all gothic to me. There was the barn dance and all sorts of awful exercises you had to do to music; there was the polka: that was fairly easy – one could generally jump around to the polka; but the waltz – I could never master that.

Overall, I suppose, education had no practical end in my case. It would never have been considered that I should get a *job*. Girls stayed at home. Many of them grew very sour over that; others adored their fathers and did everything for them.

The name of our governess was Mrs Brock and we loved her dearly from the start to the finish of her reign. For one thing, the era of luncheon in the dining-room opened for us with Mrs Brock, and with it a world of desire and satisfaction, for we were as greedy as Papa. Although governesses lunched in the dining-room, they supped on trays upstairs – that was the accepted rule, and Mummie must have been thankful for it as these luncheons meant a horrid disintegration of her times of intimacy with Papa. So much of his day was spent away from her. In the winter months he was shooting or hunting, and in the spring there was salmon fishing – all undertaken and excelled in more as a career and a duty than as the pleasures of a leisured life. In the summer months there was a horse, sometimes horses, to be got ready for the Dublin Show, often evening fishing, and always the supervision of haymaking and harvest with their attendant ghastly weather to worry him. So luncheon and dinner were, I suppose, the brightest hours in her day.

*Good Behaviour*

I suppose that my childhood is pretty well mirrored in the childhood section of *Good Behaviour*. There was the alienation between the grown-ups and the children and the consequent loneliness for the children. There was a complete division with the house – the old upstairs-downstairs thing. There were stairs for children and servants to go up and down and separate stairs for grown-ups. I was more at ease and more friendly with the maids and the farmworkers than I was with my parents.

From an early age it was instilled into one that it was important to be of 'good behaviour' at all times. Modesty was the big thing; I imagine the grown-ups feared that we would grow up rather savage otherwise.

I remember having the most appalling row with my mother over what seemed to me an innocuous incident. I was lying on the grass, kicking my legs in the air and exposing navy-blue knickers with elastic around the knees, when my mother saw me, from a window, and summoned me inside. We had a most awful row. I was very embarrassed by all this. Neither could I understand my mother's reaction to my childish abandon. I queried my sister on this much later in life and she simply said, 'Well, you know, Mother's generation just felt that modesty could not be instilled at an early enough age.' It's hard to picture that happening today, but it was a true feeling on the part of my mother: not quite Puritanism, but something that had to be absorbed by a child.

There were other traits instilled also – politeness, good manners, eating properly, table etiquette; and, of course, religion was instilled from an early age, too. Yet for all the table etiquette we only dined with our parents at lunchtime. We also had two rather tricky aunts who lived with us and they were forever correcting us. One was always being corrected for being greedy. If you dared ask for a second helping you really were frowned on: being greedy was considered a major unattractive quality in a young lady.

Papa didn't look into the schoolroom any more; and each day that came and went Mrs Brock changed before our eyes. We droned our way through our lessons; our exercise books went uncorrected; she played the piano for hours, and the sounds that came out of it were those of a wild, yearning animal. 'Broken doll – you've left behind a broken doll,' she played; and 'Where your caravan has rested, flowers I leave you on the grass'. On some days she could not face luncheon in the dining-room and had biscuits and milk in the schoolroom. I ached for her, but longed now for the happy Mrs Brock I had known; this creature was fluttering and banging itself about in a world unknown to me. Hubert and I were even driven to enjoy each other's company in preference to the wild gloom which possessed our dear friend's every mood. The birds' cages and the mouse-houses began to smell; we were never very meticulous about them, only inspired towards Mrs Brock's ideal – that they ought to smell sweet as a primrose. Now she didn't seem to care, nor about the linen; her mending days were done. 'Rubbish!' she shouted at Wild Rose. 'It's all rotten – tear it up,' and she went zipping and rending through a fine double sheet and laughed at the tatters.

It was the day when Papa came back to the schoolroom that my love for Mrs Brock was, for ever, broken and dispersed. He was a tall man, and I saw him bent over this plump little woman and heard him speaking to her in a patient, reasonable tone of voice. Tears poured over her face, her hands tried to hold on to his coat. He put her hands away from him. 'I'll take a ride with you, children, at three o'clock,' he said. 'I don't think Mrs Brock feels too well. Go and tell Hubert to get ready.'

I was dismissed, but I came back to her when I heard his step going down the wooden schoolroom stairs. 'Are you all right?' I said. She was standing at the mouse cage, looking in. She didn't answer. 'Mrs Brock?'

'Minnie's had her babies,' she said, her voice still thick from crying. 'Look – aren't they disgusting?' They were, squirming and twiddling in their nest. 'You're always asking me how they do it,' Mrs Brock went on. 'Well, I'll tell you. It's that horrible Moses: he sticks that thing of his, you must have seen it – Hubert has one too – into the hole she pees out of, and he sows the seed in her like that.'

'Oh.' I felt myself becoming heated; horrified and excited.

'That's how it happens,' Mrs Brock went on, and she gripped me by both my arms. 'That's how it happens with people too. It's a thing men do, it's all they want to do, and you won't like it.'

She still held my arms. 'Is it true?' I had to know. 'Papa and Mummie don't. They couldn't . . .'

'Oh, couldn't they?' Mrs Brock laughed and laughed. She was still laughing when I tore my arms away and ran out of the schoolroom. 'Papa's waiting for us,' I excused myself, standing for a moment in the doorway. I knew I was deserting her when she seemed to need me, as I had longed for her to need me, but I felt as frightened of her as I had of Minnie and Moses in their antics on that night when Mrs Brock had been so beflowered by happiness. When I joined Hubert and Papa in the yard I looked at him with quite new eyes. Could he and Mummie really do such a dirty thing? Was it possible? There he sat, elegant and easy on his young horse – but I knew it was true, horribly true. No wonder people kept it so secret.

*Good Behaviour*

I was only vaguely conscious of the Great War, and what it really meant. We would occasionally be summoned and told that some cousin or other had been killed in foreign fields. One put on a face of black tragedy, but you didn't really know those cousins and you didn't really know what war was like. It was a completely novel thing even to read about; and of course you didn't hear about it or see it as we do today through the media. The whole thing was very much played down anyway. The real story came out afterwards – what the young poets and others wrote and what one heard much later – but at that time there was nothing like that. They all died heroes. Nothing of the real agony and horror of war came through.

The war had another effect on the society in which I grew up, particularly on the women in that society: a whole generation of men had been practically wiped out in the war. Fortunately, in my own family my father was too old for the war and my brothers were too young. When I was growing up there was an extraordinarily high proportion of marriageable young women to men. It was a sad time for some of those women; a great many of them did not have much chance of marrying. However, I think they have grown up into happy old ladies – at least many of them that I know have done so – rather like the eternal débutante, the bridge party taking the place of the ball. But they *are* happy – just as happy as the lucky ones who had happy married lives like me.

There were of course also events happening nearer home during my childhood. I was twelve when the 1916 rebellion began. I remember hearing about the occupation of the GPO in Dublin and then everybody thinking that we were all going to be murdered. We actually built a fort on the turn of one of the avenues. I was quite frightened at the time but my sister, who was always a very courageous child, took the bread-knife to bed with her saying, 'I'm not going to take nonsense from *anybody*.' She had enormous courage but she was always using it in the wrong direction! We didn't understand at all what was going on, what anybody was fighting for – any more than, if you read any history of Ireland, how much has ever been understood at the time it happened. Eventually, when the Treaty was signed in 1921, my parents were very worried. They felt that they were being thrown to the wolves; but of course absolutely nothing ever happened. There were no wolves.

There were, I suppose, wolves of a kind later on when the Black and Tans (an irregular auxiliary force of the RIC) were around in 1919. Our house was burned down as a reprisal for some Black and Tan atrocity. It was a rather small atrocity compared with some of the other atrocities they committed; however, three big houses in the country were burned down that night. It wasn't a case of personal animosity – we were just unfortunate to be chosen as a target.

I was away at school at the time and I was very, very shocked indeed. My mother took it worse than my father. Everyone told him that he should clear out of Ireland at once, but he was absolutely determined that nothing or nobody would throw him out of Ireland. He loved the life here and he got on frightfully well with all the people about the place – and they were very fond of him. He belonged here a great deal more than lots of the hereditary Anglo-Irish did. The house was never re-built. A couple of other such houses which were being re-built were knocked down again, so my father thought it better to take a smaller compensation from the British government and he bought another smaller house next door. It was very convenient because it adjoined the land and the fishing, but it wasn't nearly as nice a house as the original one.

In my teens I began to attend the hunt with my father. It was terribly important to be good at hunting and to enjoy it – and I did enjoy it. It was a bit of life. In the early stages I went hunting one or two days a week, but later on I went a lot more frequently than that. It was very much a social occasion. If you weren't hunting or weren't any good at it, you simply didn't meet people; you didn't have any background. Hunting mattered more than anything else.

My mother never took part in the hunt, although she was an extraordinarily good judge of a horse. She gave up everything for my father. She absolutely adored him. Anyway, when they first came to Ireland from Canada she was busy having all these children. There was Walter and there was me and then there were Godfrey and Charlie – all in the space of eight years. She was absolutely immobilised!

Through the hunting I gradually met other people who were in a more advanced state of civilisation, perhaps, and I eventually broke out and joined up with them. I remember that I went down to Co. Tipperary, where there was a wonderful family by the name of Perry, and I used to spend practically half the year with them. The extraordinary thing in those days was that if a family like the Perrys fancied you, they would want you to stay with them for long periods. They would provide you with horses and everything else you needed.

Music didn't enter our lives very much. My mother had a very good ear for music but none of her children had a vestige of an ear! We never heard much music. We had no gramophone and only the governesses played the piano – but they were all rather sad dirges like 'Where Your Caravan Has Rested' and romantic songs like 'Charmaine'. The only piece of music that has a definite memory for me is Kreisler's *Caprice Viennois*. That woke latent – I'm not quite sure what! – in me.

Books played a somewhat more important part in our lives. Kipling was a tremendous favourite early on and when we were older there was a marvellous writer of romances called Dornford Yates. It was romance all the way with him and we simply loved him.

I began writing myself in my late teens. I was confined to bed with what was thought to be tuberculosis, although it was in fact some other kind of bug. I wrote an awful little hunting romance. It really was dreadful, but I suppose it was all the things I wanted to be and all the things I wanted to happen: a terribly attractive girl and smashing young men riding like mad to hounds – the lot! Incredibly, it was published but, thank God, it seems to have sunk to the bottom of nowhere by now. I hope it will never be found! I did have it published on my own initiative but I would not have admitted that I was writing at that time. It would have been considered a rather anti-social thing to do in that hunting society – a society in which I wanted to get on jolly well. I know that sounds awful but it wasn't a snob thing at all. To belong to and be accepted in such a society mattered greatly in one's life.

When our house in Co. Wexford was burned down we went to stay temporarily with some cousins in the north of Ireland. They had a fairly big house and they took us all in. I loved it there. Our cousins were so free and romantic. They had a boat and they sailed; they had gramophones and they danced after dinner. I had an absolutely marvellous time with them and then I realised that my mother was slightly disapproving of my behaviour. Awful crimes, like powdering my nose, upset her. I suppose she suddenly saw me growing up and growing away from her, but she wasn't awfully clever about the way she handled it.

I think that was the beginning of the end of childhood for me: the point where you switch from thinking that everything Mum says is right to thinking that everything Mum says is wrong. It can be a very trying time for all concerned but it has to happen. It is growth.

I don't think that I was the same kind of adult as I was a child. One changes every so often – at least if you are an uncertain character, as I am! I'm sure that I wasn't the same person that my mother knew me to be as a child, or would have wanted me to be as an adult. Even when success came to me as a writer, my mother was totally outside it. She was so terribly conscientious in her heart and mind that she didn't really approve of what I was doing.

In the first play that I wrote, I took the character of one of the old aunts who used to live with us and used that in a sort of exaggerated way as the central character. Margaret Rutherford played the part marvellously and the play was an extraordinary success, but my mother took it very badly – and why not? It *was* disloyal to twist one's own family like that but every writer uses what she knows.

I suppose that most people would say that I had a very privileged childhood but, as I have said before, although it was privileged in one sense, in many other senses it was far from privileged. It's very hard to analyse one's childhood, to divide it up in bits and pieces, as it were. I think that amusement was one of the main things that was lacking in my childhood. There wasn't very much fun, except for what one invented for oneself – and that, on the other hand, was good. Also, if lots of occupations had been devised for me I probably would have missed out on the marvellous relationship I had with the people who worked on our place. That was a very precious relationship: I simply loved them and they were wonderful to us children.

When I had children of my own I tried to learn from the lessons of my own childhood. I thought that the one thing my children must have was an enormous amount of fun and enjoyment and I fought very, very hard for that. When tragedy struck and my husband died suddenly, I think I made an awful mistake. My eldest child Sally was about six years old when her father died and she had adored him. I felt that she should have the most marvellous time, that I should give her everything to make her forget. I realise now, of course, that my approach was all wrong. I should have let her suffer and in not doing so I'm sure I tied something up inside her.

Overall, my own childhood was far from idyllic. No one ever beat me or was beastly to me – I never had *that* sort of unhappy childhood. There were certainly marvellous moments but there were also long, long periods of *boredom*, because no occupations or opportunities for fun were devised for us. Children are given occupations now, they are given a way to go; but we were left totally alone. That deprivation may have made us more inventive, but I'm not sure that the deprivation was worth going through. In my own case it made me feel that romance was far away over the hill and it probably made me search for a talent to express those feelings. The talent I discovered was writing.

# *Mary Lavin*

---

Mary Lavin was born in Massachusetts USA in 1912 and came to live in Ireland with her homesick mother when Mary was nine years old. She has been a prolific short-story writer and her many publications include *Tales from Bective Bridge*, *The Great Wave*, *Happiness*, *A Memory*, *The Shrine* and *The Stories of Mary Lavin* (Vols 1–3). Mary Lavin is now considered one of the most gifted living short-story writers and has won many awards for her work. She divides her time between her homes in Dublin and Co. Meath.

I HAVE a very bad memory. I wouldn't like to be writing or talking about the past with the need to be fully truthful. I believe in the truth of the imagination, I suppose, but I am fascinated by memory, particularly the involuntary way in which pictures from the past come before me. I know almost all my stories from beginning to end before I write them but it is only after I have written them that I recognise details from my life in the stories that I could never remember at will – a flower, the river, a landscape. The details themselves don't interest me very much, because I accept that involuntary memory is a part of creativity, but I am interested in *why* one remembers meaningless things. *Why* do I remember that little scene or part of a scene from my childhood? That never ceases to intrigue me.

Notwithstanding my poor memory, I'll try and start at the beginning. I was born in Massachusetts in the United States of America. How that came about is best illustrated in this excerpt from a semi-fictional story which I wrote about my father. The story is called 'Tom'.

My father's hair was black as the Devil's, and he flew into black, black rages. When he spoke of death, as he often did, he spoke of when he'd be put down in the black hole. You could say that everything about him was black except his red blood, his fierce blue eyes, and the gold spikes of love with which he pierced me to the heart when I was a child.

He had made a late, romantic, but not happy marriage. All the same, he and my mother stayed together their whole lives through. They drew great satisfaction to the end of their days on this earth from having kept faith with each other.

They had met on shipboard – on the *SS Franconia*. My father had gone to America when he was young, and was going back to Ireland to buy horses for the man he worked for in East Walpole, Massachusetts. My mother was returning home from a visit to a grand-aunt and grand-uncle in Waltham, where the grand-uncle was pastor of the Roman Catholic Church.

My mother's family lived in County Galway. They were not very well off. They were small-town merchants who sold coal, seeds and guano as well as tea, sugar and spirits. My mother was the eldest of twelve. It used to puzzle me that the eldest of twelve should go visiting in a land to which most Irish men and women in those days went as emigrants. Such a visit suggested refinement, and this was affirmed by her classic beauty, her waist – which was thin as the stem of a flower – her unfailing good taste, and her general manner. My father had set his eye on her the minute he went up the gangplank – she was already settled into her deck chair reading a book.

They did not marry till three years later, when, after a correspondence conducted more ardently by him than by her, he sent her a diamond ring and money for her passage out again – this time to marry him. They were married from the parochial house in Waltham.

My mother hated living in America, and on three occasions when my father let her go to see her people he had to follow and fetch her home. When she spoke of her ocean crossings, whichever way she was going, my mother referred to them all as visits, until the last one, when, eastward bound and taking me with her, she knew she'd never have to go back. My father had drawn out some of his savings and given her money to buy a house in Ireland. She bought it in Dublin. Then he gave up his job, took the rest of his money out of the bank, and went to Ireland himself – for good.

'Tom' from *The Shrine and other stories*

My mother hated America; so much so that she wanted to go back to Ireland straight after the marriage. She became pregnant with me, however, and was not allowed to travel. The Cunard Line would not allow a pregnant woman to travel – which was ironic, because many pregnant women travelled the other way, from Ireland to America, and many children were

*1. The young Maeve Binchy.*

*2. Maeve Binchy.*

*3. Clare Boylan on her First Communion Day.*

*4. Clare Boylan.*

*Four of the Devlin sisters as children:* (left to right) *Polly, Marie, Val and Anne.*

*Polly Devlin.*

7. The young Jennifer Johnston with her mother, Shelah Richards – and friend.

8. Jennifer Johnston.

9. (Facing page) Molly Keane.

10. (Facing page) *Mary Lavin.*

11. *The young Joan Lingard and her dog.*

12. *Joan Lingard.*

*13. Dervla Murphy with her bicycle.*

*14. Edna O'Brien.*

actually born on board ship to Irish emigrants. My mother was eventually allowed to go when she had weaned me – I was about six months old. My father let her go back home 'for a visit' but he had to follow her to get her back to America. We spent about two years in Ireland then and I think my mother eventually only went back to pack things up and persuade my father to come home for good. However, she had another little misadventure then: the First World War broke out and, what with passport and political difficulties, she was detained in America for another seven years, before we returned to Ireland for good when I was nine.

East Walpole, Massachusetts, was a lovely place to grow up. Our house was quite an ordinary house on the banks of the Naponsett river; and behind it there were large woods, part of the demesne owned by a mill-owner for whom my father worked. I spent a lot of my time wandering through the woods. I had a particular passion for flowers and I remember the excitement of finding a yellow violet. I knew all about blue and white violets, but a yellow violet seemed very exotic to me.

I was an only child but I was never in the least lonely. I enjoyed solitude but I was also gregarious, and I had great fun at school with my companions. Books were also my great companions, although, try as I can, I cannot remember any books in our house except *Pears Cyclopaedia*, which I read over and over again. My father had very little education and his reading did not extend beyond the newspaper. My mother read a great deal – mostly novelettas of romantic fiction, of the kind that Victorian ladies in Galway enjoyed. She joined the library when she went to live in East Walpole and she enrolled me at a young age. I must have been a voracious reader because I remember the librarian, Miss Childs (how strange that I remember *her* name after all those years!), saying to my mother, 'I'm afraid that Mary has read everything in the children's library. We have nothing more to give her.' I had to be allowed into the adult section where I read quite a lot of adult books – very carefully chosen by Miss Childs of course! I remember reading *The House of Seven Gables* and, of course,

*Hiawatha*, which I memorised and loved to recite as I walked through the woods thinking I was Hiawatha. When I went back to Ireland at the age of nine I found that the children there were only reading school stories. Children don't like to be different of course, so I dropped all the reading I had done in America and began to read what the Irish children were reading.

Although my father had a deep and a strong mind, and was the subtlest human being I ever knew, he had had small schooling. He could read and write, but with difficulty. He came, indeed, from stock that had in the penal days produced a famous hedge schoolmaster, and of this he was very proud. It may well have been his pride in this scholarly kinsman that led to his own premature departure from a one-room schoolhouse in Frenchpark.

For, one day the schoolmaster, in a poetic discourse on spring, invoked the cuckoo, and made reference to the cuckoo's nest.

My father's hand flew up, and without waiting for permission to speak, he gave voice to his shock and indignation. 'The cuckoo doesn't build a nest! She lays her eggs in another bird's nest!'

'Is that so?' The master must have been sorely nettled by this public correction. 'Well boy, if you think you can teach this class better than me, come up to the blackboard and take my place.' Then, abandoning sarcasm, he roared and caught up his cane. 'I'll teach you not to interrupt me!' he cried.

'You're wrong there, too,' my father said. 'You'll teach me nothing more as long as you live.' And with that he picked up his slate and fired it at the master's head. Fortunately, for once his aim was bad, and he missed. Instead, he put a gash an inch deep in the blackboard, and in the hullabaloo he lit out of the door and down the road for Dublin. He was in such a rage he forgot to say goodbye to his mother, whom he never saw again in this life.

From Dublin my father went to Liverpool; from there to the potato fields in Scotland and the hop fields in Yorkshire; and, finally, one Palm Sunday morning, he arrived in Boston, then a leading port. All he took with him to America were the memories of the boy he had been, running barefoot over the bogs and the unfenced fields of Roscommon with a homemade fishing rod in his hand, or maybe a catapult. That boy used to think nothing of running across country from Castlerea to Boyle, and even into Sligo. Towns that lay twenty miles apart were no distance to him –

leaping stone walls like a young goat, bounding over streams like a hound, and taking the corner off a lake if there was a wind to dry out his clothes. Whenever I think of what it is to be young, I find my mind invaded by images of a boy – a boy running over unpeopled land under a sky filled with birds. My father had made his memories mine.

'Tom' from *The Shrine and other stories*

I loved my father very, very dearly. I think that he was well worth loving because I still meet people who tell me what an extraordinary person he was. To me he was a heroic figure and the only genius I ever knew.

He was fifty-one when I was born and, while I was not conscious of his age in an abstract way, I remember seeing him bathing at the seaside once and when I saw him with all the other fathers, I got a tremendous intuition that he was older than them and it gave me a terrible fright. That fright could have led to having a special love for him; on the other hand, it could have led to the obsession with death which people say runs through my work.

I have also a tremendous passion for the sea (although I have never lived by the sea) and again it is linked to my father and those 'gold spikes with which he pierced me to the heart'. When my mother and I returned to Ireland on the SS *Wine-friedian* and I saw my father drive away in a beachwagon it was a lonely feeling, even though I knew we would see him again. But travelling across the Atlantic ocean brought home the vastness of the gulf between my father and me; and all the time the sea was entering into my feelings as a powerful emotion. Later, when I stood on the beach in Galway, I had no interest in sandcastles. I just stood there, spellbound by that great stretch of water which separated me from my father.

I always assume that any gifts I have inherited came from my father because of the real depth and power of his emotion. He was such a strong person and yet, looking back on it, I think that I may be unjust to my mother, because I thought of her as a rather giddy little person, full of stories. She was always telling me stories of her own childhood. Unlike me she had a great memory. There was simply nothing she forgot about her childhood and later, when I came to write, I think I drew on *her* memories. Her memories seemed to become more real than my own.

I suppose she was an unhappy person – she may even have been unhappy at home. I remember her telling me that she was always called 'Miss Imperious' as a young girl. I have an old photograph at home of a church picnic group. The group is arranged in front of an old abbey but my mother has found herself a niche in the abbey wall and, standing there in that niche, she certainly looks the part of 'Miss Imperious'.

I never got to know my mother as well as I knew my father, which is very sad. As I grew older, we had less in common. We got on very well, however. There was none of this generation gap that we hear about nowadays. When I got very much older – you might even say *old* – and my mother was very old, I found that being an only child was the greatest curse that could befall a person because I had this very old mother and nobody to share the burden of looking after her. Generally we got on very well but to me she never seemed to be the worthwhile figure that my father was. I feel bad about that.

My mother eventually got her way about 'visiting' and returned with me to her native place – Athenry, Co. Galway. I had a rather curious existence there. We were supposed to be going back to America in a month or two so I did not go to school there initially. But we actually spent eight months there and for the first six months I didn't go to school. I was having a solitary life again – solitary but not lonely. Instead of the trees and flowers of Massachusetts I now had the company of *people*, which was new to me.

Even in my own mother's home there were so many people. She was the eldest of twelve children and most of them were at home, so I had this large extended family. Then there was the family shop which meant that I met a lot more people. Outside the home and the shop, I was a great wanderer. I would wander all over the town and of course, having come from America, I was a real *persona grata*. I was in everybody's house, having barmbrack and cake and lemonade. They were probably asking me a lot of questions about my family, questions which I was only too ready to answer, but equally I was seeing the intimate side of their lives – all the rows, the love affairs, the jealousies and whatever. I was taking in all this, although I didn't realise it at the time.

Later, when I began to write, this period in Athenry was to influence me greatly. I had never intended to be a writer. I had written a book or two early on, including a school story when I was about fourteen. But it was really only for *fun* – I was a bit of a show-off at the time.

However, some American critic found out about it and saw it somewhere. He insisted that I had an instinct for writing at an early age, which is quite ridiculous because I also illustrated the story and I had no more wish to be an artist than I had to be a writer. It was the type of thing that many adolescents write – my attic at home is full of 'books' written by my own children and my grandchildren. I think the sad thing is that some children begin to write at that stage and perhaps their parents or somebody else encourages them; they then think that they are writers and they continue writing, which is a great pity.

But later when I came to write a story about an aunt of mine in Athenry, all of a sudden I knew that I had a facile gift. I had always been very good at essays in school and I knew that I could write; but I hadn't realised the power there is in writing and how much I could extract out of myself by writing. I realised how much there was that I didn't know I knew until I began to write, and when I began to write it came out in a kind of involuntary way. When I wrote I cast the characters in the mould of the people in Athenry. I used them as prototypes for people like them that I had met elsewhere.

I am told that I was a very good little girl when I lived in Massachusetts – I suppose you can't get into very much trouble wandering through the woods and along the river bank – but when I wandered around Athenry I grew very naughty very quickly! Finally my uncles told my mother that it didn't matter how long or short a time I was staying, I was to be got off the streets of Athenry and out of the houses. So I was sent to the convent school.

I loved it there. It was so different, so strange. Every town child brought a penny to keep the school fire going and the country children brought a sod of turf instead of a penny. I remember distinctly what a stigma there was attached to those who brought the turf. I think that children have a great sense of justice; certainly I had a very early sense of justice. In my childish way I thought it extraordinary that children were looked down on for bringing in a sod of turf because people were always giving me pennies but they never gave me sods of turf.

My father eventually had to accede to my mother's wishes and come back to Ireland, but by an extraordinary twist of fate he was employed over here by the same family whom he worked for in America. He had become a very close friend of the son of his employer and when that son came to visit my father they took a drive around Ireland. They happened to drive through a derelict estate in Bective, Co. Meath – an estate of some three hundred acres, two thirds of which were woodlands.

'Why don't you buy that estate and I will run it for you?' said my father. The son did buy it and my father ran it as estate manager. He was a very astute cattleman and had a great knowledge of horses. He bought Workman, which was later to win the Grand National. He would sell such horses to someone who could afford to train them – and for the same amount which he had paid. He knew that those horses were winners and he just wanted to see them win.

My parents were not happy with each other. I have no real reason for saying that, except a kind of intuition. Certainly they managed not to be in the same house very often. My father was on the estate in Bective, while my mother was in the house in Dublin which they had bought as a compromise for her. Based with my mother in Dublin, but visiting my father regularly, I had the best of both worlds. I loved Bective but I loved Dublin too. We lived near Leeson Street Bridge and I spent a great deal of my time wandering all over the city (something a child couldn't do today) through the Liberties (old Dublin), along the quays, out to the Bull Wall. I don't know how I was allowed so much liberty but my childhood was certainly a wandering one.

Living in Dublin also meant that I could go to day school rather than boarding school. I went to Loreto Convent School in St Stephen's Green. I was so happy there. I loved it for a variety of reasons. I did well academically; being a gregarious type I loved meeting and mixing with other girls; also, I suppose there wasn't a great intellectual stimulus at home, so I responded readily to the challenge of school. At the same time I was not unduly forced to study at home.

I was a good all-rounder at school. My father had been a champion athlete in Co. Roscommon (or 'champeen', as they would say). The Loreto order had a big sports day for all their schools at which I picked up quite a lot of medals for running and jumping. My father always came to the sports – he loved to see me excel at sport.

He would come to the school at other times too. He wanted me to be well educated; he would always say 'I want you to go to college, Mary, not like me.' But he would have no qualms either about walking into the school and taking me to Aintree for two or three days. The nuns were all terrified of him, because he would come in and call for Reverend Mother and say to her, 'I want to take Mary out for the day. It's a lovely fine day and I don't see why she should be cooped up in here!'

Leaving America and coming to live in Ireland had been a 'culture shock' in many ways (even for a nine-year-old) but particularly so with respect to religion and its practice. When we lived in that small town only thirteen miles from Boston we had Mass in the local movie house. On Saturday night after the final performance the screen was taken down and the altar put up in readiness for Sunday Mass. If for any reason the priest couldn't come, we went to the Greek Orthodox Church or the Polish Church with full permission.

When I came to Ireland, however, religion (and *one* religion at that) was all-pervasive. Everyone was always rushing off not just to Mass but to Benediction and the Stations of the Cross. Religion was a very big part of those eight months in Athenry. I became intrigued by graveyards – I hadn't ever been in a graveyard before. I found that the church itself was an absolutely wonderful place to play – among the pews and in the confessionals, running in and out behind the statues and shrines. It was probably when I was discovered at this that I was sent to school.

I had a tremendous time during those eight months; but when I grew older I suffered very, very deeply from scruples, from worries about imagined sins. I should have been more intelligent about it all, because I did win a bishop's medal for catechism. But although I suffered, I was able ultimately to shake the scrupulousness off. It didn't bother me. I didn't feel that I had to throw away everything; I kept a few basic beliefs. In fact, that era gave me a great sense of conscience, and of the power and beauty of private conscience – something I believe in absolutely. I find it hard to understand some Irish writers who claim that their lives were destroyed by some little sex exploits or imagined sins when they were children; I find it hard to understand that they were so brittle.

I think my childhood was probably idyllic in America and in Ireland it was great fun; but there was a very dark side to that fun. For instance, I recall being so bored at Benediction one day that for something to do I began to pick off the paintbrush hairs that had been embedded in the whitewashed walls of the church. I found this a great distraction and I amassed a great collection of hairs which I brought home. An aunt of mine nearly had a fit when she saw them and sent me right back to put them back on the church wall, claiming that I had committed a sin by stealing from God's house. Later, when I grew older, things like that, combined with the study of catechism, were the cause of unhappiness to me in adolescence; but there again that unhappiness didn't hurt me in the long term. I don't really resent those events, nor do I feel that any of those things made my life in any way odd or unhappy.

By and large, then, my childhood was a happy one. There

was no dramatically sudden end to it. In a curious way, I slipped out of the solitude and beauty of childhood into the books which touched on what I felt and thought; and through those books I progressed to adulthood. One day I read *Adam Bede* by chance and that was the end of the school stories that I had been reading. I loved the Russian writers and later when I was at college I grew to love French literature, particularly Racine, not so much for the content as for the technique. I became tremendously interested in technique, in the music and architecture of words. It was thus through reading that I passed from childhood to adulthood.

# Joan Lingard

Joan Lingard was born in Edinburgh but spent practically all of her childhood in Belfast. Although she has written many novels for adults, Joan Lingard is probably better known as a children's novelist, particularly for the quintet of books which grew out of the conflict in Northern Ireland in 1969. Those five books – *The Twelfth Day of July*, *Across the Barricades*, *Into Exile*, *A Proper Place* and *Hostages to Fortune* – follow the destinies of Sadie, a Protestant girl and Kevin, a Catholic boy from childhood to maturity. Joan Lingard has also written the 'Maggie' books about Glaswegian, Maggie McKinley, and she has adapted these for television. Her publications for adults include *Reasonable Doubts* and *Sisters by Rite* – the latter being partly autobiographical. Joan Lingard now lives in Edinburgh and spends part of the year in Canada.

Although I was born in Edinburgh, my childhood really belongs to Belfast, to which our family moved when I was two years old. My father was in the Royal Navy Reserve Service and he went to work on a training ship called the *Caroline* which was docked in Belfast. When the war broke out he was recalled to active service but he stayed in Belfast and worked around the docks.

My very earliest memory of Belfast is of the street we went to live in which was off the Newtownards Road in East Belfast. The houses were still being built and I remember the workmen calling after me as I rode past them on my tricycle. They were probably just being friendly but I was very frightened of them and the memory of that fear abides with me . . .

The particular area where we lived was a Protestant stronghold with just a few Catholics around, but I was of neither denomination, being a Christian Scientist – which was perhaps a very odd thing to be in Belfast, although there were quite a number of minority sects in the city. Growing up, I felt very much an outsider, because my friends were either Presbyterian, Church of Ireland or Methodist and each denomination seemed to me to feel a superiority over the other one. I became very much aware that all these denominations mattered greatly and here was I belonging to none of them.

Being a Christian Scientist wasn't really a family thing. I was taken to the Church first when I was about five by my friend's parents, who were Christian Scientists. My mother went to the Church but she was not a member. My father never went at all, except for the Sunday after my mother died, because he felt that she would have liked that.

The Christian Scientists were founded by Mary Baker Eddy over a hundred years ago in Boston, Massachusetts. One of their basic tenets is that there is no sin, disease or death. That is a very difficult tenet to grow up with, because you later discover that there is an awful lot of sin, disease and death around – and that is difficult to come to terms with. The Christian Scientists don't believe in having doctors. If anyone is ill you 'work at it' – i.e. you read the Bible and Mary Baker Eddy's *Science and Health with Key to the Scriptures*; and, of course, very often cures do take place because so much illness is psychological. It's a question of mind over matter.

I grew up accepting the Christian Science beliefs and I was really very happy within the Church. I was very immersed in Christian Science; I read from *Science and Health* every day as we were required to do. I didn't find it a chore – but that is not to say I was totally pious either! At the age of twelve I joined the Mother Church in Boston, which appealed greatly to me at the time because I saw myself going to Boston at some point in the future.

I loved the church in Belfast. It was white with a blue ceiling and there was a tremendous feeling of lightness and sunlight there. Everyone was very cheerful and happy, and there was no talk of the wrath of God. God was good and everyone was happy – so I really did enjoy Sundays! Christian Science was threaded through my life, or rather through part of my life because I actually led a double life: one in the street or school with my friends and another different life in church where the happy atmosphere seemed at odds with other religions. As someone once said to me, 'You're not a real Protestant at all.'

I had one sister who was eleven years older than me and when she went to work in London I was to all intents an only child, growing up with my mother. My father seemed to be away from home a lot and I didn't have a very close relationship with him as a child. I don't think that he was very good with young children and he left my mother to lead a quiet life at home. I had no extended family at all. I had to rely on friends or neighbours on the street, so I suppose in some ways I was rather a lonely child, although I always seemed to have lots to do. Perhaps that is partly why I became a writer, because if you are born in the midst of a large and noisy family, there is always something clamouring for your attention and you don't have the peace or the time to write.

I had a very happy and close relationship with my mother. She was a very good person. I don't think that I ever saw her in any kind of rage or being unfair to anyone. I never went through the adolescent period of rebellion against my mother. I have three daughters of my own and I have been through it all with them. They don't exactly turn against you but they work out a lot of their adolescent problems, using you like a punch-bag. I could never have done that with my mother, but that may have been because she was ill during my adolescence. She developed cancer and she died when I was sixteen.

That was the greatest trauma of my life. It has influenced my whole life, even to the extent that when each of my daughters turned sixteen I was worried in case something should happen to me and that they would have to go through what I had gone through. My mother's death had a tremendous effect on me. I once heard Laurence Olivier say that his mother died when he was very young – twelve I think – and he never recovered from it. I know what he meant. It is not that one goes around feeling gloomy all the time, but it leaves its mark.

I think that my mother's death was also the beginning of the end of my belief in Christian Science. I stayed with it until I eventually rejected it when I was eighteen. I still think that some of the things I learned as a child hold true – but certainly not the belief that there is no sin, disease or death. Rejecting Christian Science was the second great trauma in my life. I was rejecting not only a religion but also a way of life; I had made many friends through Christian Science and my rejecting it meant the end of those friendships.

When my mother died, I was thrown together with my father for a while (he returned to Edinburgh a short time later), and I got to know him a bit more, but it was my mother who had been closest to me and who mattered most in my life.

The children in our neighbourhood mixed pretty well because they were mostly of one persuasion. We had one Catholic family three or four doors down from us and my mother was very friendly with them – in fact when my mother died, we gave her clothes to the Catholic mother – but of course we went to separate schools and I really grew up not having many Catholic friends. I was aware very early on of the segregation because I was a Christian Scientist and because my mother did not subscribe to segregation.

We were holding our sides with laughter when the door scraped open and Rosie put her head in.

'You should be ashamed of yourself so you should, Cora Caldwell, playing shops with a dirty Fenian lavvy brush!' She faced Teresa. 'If I'd a penny do you know what I'd do? I'd buy a rope and hang the Pope and let King Billy through!'

The travelling rug was flung aside, and in one wild leap Teresa was across the floor and had hold of Rosie's fair curls. Rosie screamed and took a handful of Teresa's black ones. They held tight. They let their voices soar.

Before long my mother arrived on a peace mission.

'Girls, girls . . .' She forced them apart, kept them firmly at bay. They snarled and spat and aimed kicks behind her back. I could tell that she was knowing the Truth about them, reciting inside her head that they were God's children made in God's image. Heaving and panting, they subsided. Teresa's dress was torn from shoulder to waist. Spittle ran down Rosie's cheek. My mother took their hands and let them into the house. I straightened the toothbrushes, put out the light and went in after them.

They sat one on either side of the fireplace scowling down at their laps while my mother read to them from her book with the gold cross and crown on the cover. ' *"Divine love always has met and always will meet every human need . . ."* ' Her voice, soft and gentle, flowed on, mingling with the soothing crackle of the fire, and gradually the scowls faded and the lines were straightened out just as they had been on the ould fella's face after death. She read for a long time and when she closed the book she said, 'Be at peace with one another, children. There is enough violence in the world as it is.' Then she made us cocoa and jam sandwiches with Veda bread and went upstairs to find an old dress of mine for Teresa.

Next day at school Rosie said, 'Your mother's a queer turn so she is.' No queerer than her lot with their Orange singing! 'Oh, all right, Cora, I wasn't meaning nothing.' We were friends again, promenading round the playground, arms linked, sharing our playpieces.

*Sisters by Rite*

*Sisters by Rite* contains a lot of autobiographical material, but that is not to say that it is an autobiography. The central character, Cora, is an only child and a Christian Scientist. She lives in a street very like the street I lived in and she goes to a school very like the school I went to – but I wasn't Cora! I have used the raw material and changed things around somewhat. The book is set in the war years, and even then there were sectarian tensions, particularly when a Catholic family moved into the street.

The McGills were discussing the new occupants of Number Thirteen.
  'It'll be the ruination of the street,' said Uncle Billy.
  'Imagine – Taigs!'
  'Maybe they won't stay long,' I said. 'They might not like it.'
  'Aye, they might not, Cora.' Uncle Billy gave me a nod of approval.
  'I just hope there'll be no trouble, that's all,' said Granny McGill.
  'Why would there be?' I asked.
  'You can't blame people for having strong feelings can you?' I supposed not, though I was not sure.
  'Their ways are not our ways, know what I mean?' I didn't but knew that I was not meant to say so. 'And they wouldn't want us in their streets, would they?'
  'The devil they wouldn't,' said Uncle Billy.
  'Like should stick with like,' said Granny McGill. 'That way there's less trouble.'

*Sisters by Rite*

I suppose that in a predominantly Protestant street the Protestants felt the status quo was threatened and were not very pleased at Catholics moving in. That is not to say that they were all like that – it was mostly the extremists who resented the intrusion. 'Uncle Billy' would probably be a follower of Ian Paisley today.

As children we played a lot in the streets – skipping, swinging around the lampposts and playing a lot of 'pretend' games in sheds and garages. We made up many more games than my own children did. Whenever there was a building site – maybe another street going up – we played there a great deal, having tremendous fun with the bricks – building one's own city, as it were.

The twelfth of July was of course an occasion of great excitement on the streets. The noise of the drums, the sound of marching feet, the rousing music of the bands, the huge colourful banners – all of these made the Orange parades very exciting for a child to watch. My mother didn't like the parades at all and, as I later realised, Catholics obviously didn't particularly enjoy them; but as a young child they were a source of great enjoyment for me.

They were coming! I stood in the gutter and leant out from the waist to get a better view. Rosie forgot her scuffed shoe. First came the huge banner of the Lodge carried aloft by Uncle Billy and Uncle Sam and two other stout-armed men. Four small boys held on to its tasselled stays for dear life in case the wind would take a swipe at it. The hand-painted picture of the man in the plumed hat and the white horse rippled. 'LONG LIVE KING BILLY', the slogan said above it. And 'THIS WE WILL MAINTAIN', underneath. We waved and we cheered. The uncles never looked sideways. The drum major drew level, dazzling our eyes as he tossed his baton high over his head, twirled it behind his back, and now he was turning himself round and round, and all the while the baton was on the go, whirling, birling, rising, falling. And then the drummer with his drum so large I was amazed he could get his arms right round it. And what a sight it was, all decorated in scarlet, orange and gold! I longed to play a Lambeg drum. The band followed tootling on their flutes and banging on their drums. Deanna's father was playing the trumpet just like Louis Armstrong. Deanna waved frantically and got her fur-fringed bolero in a twist.

'Sure isn't this just good fun, Cora?' said Mrs Meneely. 'I don't know what your mother could object to. Plenty RCs come out to watch and all.'

At last came the dark-suited men of the Lodge walking two abreast, their arms swinging, their feet moving in time (more or less) to the music. Some of them carried rolled black umbrellas like lances in front of them. I glanced up at the sky but there was no sign of rain. It was tradition, said Granny McGill, to remind you of the days when the Orangemen had had to defend themselves with whatever came to hand.

Rosie and her family had to wait for a car which would pick them up and take them to the 'Field' where they would eat, drink and be merry, play games and listen to speeches. I left them and ran beside the uncles' Lodge for a long way, going quite close to the city centre which I was not allowed to do alone. When I tired I turned and walked the other way. Wave after wave of men passed me with banners, fifes and drums. I enjoyed the pictures on the banners which depicted scenes from Irish history (Prods triumphing of course) and some from English, such as a turbanned black man giving a box of jewels to Queen Victoria and her Albert. I didn't understand the caption: 'THE SECRET OF ENGLAND'S GREATNESS.' The slogans bemused me 'TRUST IN GOD AND KEEP YOUR POWDER DRY.' 'CEMENTED WITH LOVE.' 'NO SURRENDER.' I knew that one well enough and knew what it meant.

The marching men would never surrender, nor tire either. They wouldn't need to for they hadn't even started on the parade proper, were only on their way to the rallying point at Carlisle Circus where they would meet up with Lodges from all over the city and province. They looked as if they could have walked the length of Ireland.

And now the men were behind me. The sound of the music was diminishing. Rosie and Deanna waved from the rear window of a car. Walking backwards, I watched the flip-flap of their hands working like frantic windscreen wipers. Then they, too, were gone.

In the streets behind the main road it was like Sunday. A piece of rope dangled from the lamppost at the corner of our street. Putting the loop under my bottom I swung idly to and fro wondering how to fill the long hours before Rosie would come back and tell me everything. Teresa had gone to stay with an aunt on the Falls for a few days.

*Sisters by Rite*

I was absolutely crazy about books. They fascinated me. I could never get enough to read and I am sure that is why I ultimately became a writer. The local library was quite far away, so I couldn't go there on my own when I was young. It appeared to me then to be like an old shed; and in fact when I went back there again recently it still looked like that! The books then were very tattered and ancient. They had long since lost their dust jackets and their spines had a greasy feeling about them. The pages were filthy, spattered with egg and tomato ketchup. I hated the feel of those books so much that I used to turn the pages with a postcard and cover the spine with a paper wrapper – but that didn't thwart my love of the books themselves. I read absolutely everything I was allowed to read in the junior library – you weren't allowed into the senior section until you were fourteen. I read all the books that children have loved for years – the 'Chalet School' books, Enid Blyton, *Just William*, *Biggles* – and when my mother would ask me what I wanted for Christmas I always demanded a book. One Christmas I got eight books and I had read them all before I went to bed that night! My mother was beginning to despair of keeping me supplied with books and finally one day, when I was moaning, 'I've got nothing to read, I'm bored!', she turned to me and said, 'Why don't you go away and write your own books?' That was how I began as a writer, at the age of eleven.

I got some lined foolscap paper, filled my fountain pen with green ink (because I thought that was a very suitable colour for a writer!) and sat down to write my first book. It was about a girl called Gail. It was one of those books in which a telegram arrives calling the parents away to somewhere like Rangoon ('Great Aunt Emily very ill. Come at once!'). Gail was sent to her grandmother in Cornwall where she found a smugglers' cave which led to various secret passages ... Eventually she tracked down the smugglers and was confronted by a villain with scars zig-zagging down his face to the corners of his mouth. It was very unsubtle characterisation: he might as well have had a placard on his chest saying, 'I am the villain'! In the end Gail brings the smugglers to justice and – lo and behold! – her uncle Bill appears on the scene and he happens to be a detective who has been trying to track the smugglers down for years without success. There were definitely shades of Enid Blyton lurking in the background!

I wasn't happy with my 'book' in loose sheets. I wanted to make a real book, so I copied the whole story out in my best writing in an exercise book (in blue ink this time). I made a dust-wrapper, illustrated it and wrote a 'blurb'. I wrote 'Books by Joan Lingard' on the back, then under it 'No. 1 – *Gail*' and at the bottom 'Published by Lingard & Co.' That was my first publication!

Other books were to follow in this series, 'Books by Joan Lingard'. I wrote *The Further Adventures of Gail* and another book was *The Strange House on the Moors*. The latter was a story about twin girls of fourteen and it was set on the Yorkshire moors. I remember painting the twins on the cover. They had long blonde hair in plaits down to the waist. (There was a certain amount of wish-fulfilment in that: I had always wanted to grow my hair long but my mother wouldn't allow it, in case I picked up lice in school. She insisted on a pudding-bowl style.) The twins arrived on the moors on a wild stormy night and a big mansion loomed up before them. The door opened and an evil-looking housekeeper invited them in . . . I think that by then I would have been reading the Brontës!

I wrote at that time mainly for my own gratification. I showed the books to my best friend and to my mother, but I don't think my father was very interested in them. I doubt if he ever saw them. He liked me to do well at school but that was the limit of his interest. He never came to the prize-giving at school, for example.

I went to the Strandtown Primary School – or Public Elementary School, as it was then called. I wasn't particularly happy there – happy in patches, maybe, but I was very shy as a young girl and I don't think that I ever quite found my feet in primary school. When I went to secondary school – Bloomfield Collegiate – at eleven, I really enjoyed my time there.

Bloomfield Collegiate was a very small school in an old building and it was run on fairly antediluvian lines. The classes were small, and it hadn't a great academic record, but I enjoyed it. Its eccentricity appealed to me much more than a large well-run school would have done and I made a lot of very good friends there.

In fact, there were eight of us who were known as 'the gang', and we were constantly getting into trouble. Bloomfield had some sort of connection then with the local Presbyterian Church and, due to lack of space, our form was housed in the church hall. We had one or two teachers who weren't very good at keeping control, so we would slip out and go into the church and preach sermons to one another. We played football in the church garden and walked round the edge of a static water-tank pretending we were circus performers.

We were terrible miscreants, really, but a lot of things that I have written about have come out of that time. I wrote a children's book called *The File on Fraulein Berg* based on a German teacher we had at Bloomfield. We thought she was a German spy and we followed her all over Belfast noting her movements in a notebook. One morning she came into our class and said, 'Isn't it wonderful? Paris has been liberated!' We suddenly realised that she was on our side. Not long afterwards she left the school and we heard that she had gone to Palestine. We learned then that she was Jewish. We hadn't realised that and we had been horrible to her.

I am still very friendly with 'the gang'. We keep in touch with one another, even though we are now widely spread, from Belfast itself, England and Scotland to Eastern Canada and Vancouver. I keep in touch with them all because they were and are important to me.

My memory of Belfast is very much coloured by the war, which impinged a lot on my childhood. I remember the blackout in particular, the air-raid shelters and coming home with a torch, worrying about the dark. Belfast was the city of dark for me at that time, whereas Dublin became the city of light. My mother and I went to Dublin on shopping trips – mostly buying very inexpensive things, I might add, things like chocolate and butter and zips, which you couldn't get in

Belfast. We used to sew them inside the linings of our coats so that they wouldn't be found by the customs officers. There was excitement in doing the forbidden; but even greater was the excitement of Dublin itself. There was a wonderful atmosphere in the air. All the lights were on and the shops were full of magic things. Dublin was for me a marvellous city.

We stepped into the streets of Dublin. The bright lights astounded me.

'It's like daytime.'

'This is what it'll be like in Belfast,' said Aunt Belle, 'when the lights come on again.'

But I knew that it could never be quite like this. There was an excitement about the city that made me want to skip. The streets swarmed with people who looked as if they were enjoying themselves. Pub doors swung open spilling out light and noise. The restaurants were busy, the shop windows full. I was enthralled.

I told Rosie that I was going to live in Dublin when I grew up.

'But what about the nuns and priests?'

I hadn't noticed that many.

'Not noticed them? You must need glasses, Cora Caldwell!'

There had been so many other things to do, I retorted, like eating knickerbocker glories in Cafollas, drinking tea in Bewley's Oriental Tea Room, shopping in O'Connell Street, walking in the Phoenix Park, taking the tram to Dun Laoghaire and walking along the sea front; and there had been so many other things to look at, like chocolates piled up on shop counters, pounds and pounds of them, and silk stockings and diamond rings.

The night before we came home we sat in our hotel room sewing labels from Robinson and Cleaver's and Anderson and MacAuley's into our new clothes. My mother sprinkled a little talcum powder over them, so that the materials wouldn't look so new. 'There now!' She admired a green corduroy dress she'd bought for me. 'You'd never know, would you?'

*Sisters by Rite*

Apart from books, my other great sources of entertainment as a child were the cinema and the radio. We girls went at least once a week to the Astoria cinema, where the programme changed twice weekly. It was cheap to go to the cinema in those days and we were very much sold on the 'American dream'. Our minds were taken up with what it would be like to live like Esther Williams in a huge apartment with a swimming pool and to wear a white swimming costume with flowers in your hair ... America was very much the pool of life that one wanted to jump into.

In those pre-television days I listened a lot to the radio – *Children's Hour* at five o'clock every afternoon, serials like *The Swish of the Curtain* and *Paul Temple*. We would discuss each episode the following morning in school, so I suppose all of those things fed the imagination greatly.

I always wanted to be a writer. I didn't ever admit to it, because I felt self-conscious about it. I didn't know anyone who was one; I didn't meet a writer until my first book was accepted for publication. I was fourteen when I had finished the fourth book 'published by Lingard & Co.' and after that I entered the self-conscious adolescent stage, where you have a lot of ideas and you begin writing something, then when you get to about page thirty you say 'This is a load of rubbish' and you throw it into a drawer. I suppose also that I didn't have much time to write, with so many other things to do and my mother being ill. But the desire to write – and to write *novels* – never left me.

I wrote first for adults. My first book, *Liam's Daughter*, was published in 1962. It was set in Northern Ireland and in France but the characters were Irish and they were characters I could understand. My early unpublished 'books' were written from second- and third-hand experience and I eventually realised that I would write successfully only if I wrote about the people and the backgrounds that I knew and understood. I wrote six novels in that early phase.

I didn't really consider writing for children until the last of those six was published. It was called *The Lord on Our Side* and it was about Ulster from the 1940s to the 1960s. A friend of mine, Honor Arundel, who was a children's writer, read that book and said, 'Why don't you write a book *for children* about what is happening in Northern Ireland *now*?' (This was 1969 when the present troubles were starting up.) I realised then that there was a book waiting inside my head – all I needed was for someone to press the button and say 'Do that' and it happened. I had a Protestant girl called Josie in *The Lord on Our Side*. I changed her into Sadie and I created a Catholic boy called Kevin as a balance to her. They lived very close to one another and I set the story in the days leading up to the twelfth of July. Kevin and Sadie are, of course, on opposite sides until they meet and develop a liking for each other ... In a way, *The Twelfth Day of July* seemed to write itself. It came very easily to me and I intended to write only that one book; but Kevin and Sadie had got such a hold of my imagination that I couldn't leave them alone. I went on to write *Across the Barricades* and the other three books in the series. I had become a children's writer almost by accident.

When I wrote those five books for children, my aim was to be completely impartial, and my Christian Science upbringing certainly helped me, in that I was detached from both sides; also, because I had left Belfast I wasn't sucked into it emotionally and therefore I could be more objective about it.

Obviously my childhood has influenced all my writing. I really believe that the first eighteen years lay down almost everything. The more I go on the more I draw from my childhood. It seems like a well that grows deeper and deeper the more I lower the bucket into it.

I stayed on in Belfast for two years after my mother's death. My father in fact left Belfast after a year and moved back to Edinburgh. I stayed with a friend and left school when I had done my Senior Certificate. I took a job in the Ulster Bank but I was very unsettled. I really couldn't go on living in someone else's house, although they were very kind to me. I suppose I felt a need to go back and see my mother's home town of Edinburgh, so I went over and got a job in the public library before deciding to train as a teacher, and I moved back with my father while I trained.

Belfast still means friendship to me. I like going back for visits because I enjoy seeing my friends, who are extremely hospitable. At the same time, when I walk through the streets I feel very sad that the city should be so divided and so stained with trouble. I feel sad because I don't see how it is ever going to change, although I am amazed by the resilience and cheerfulness of the people. They try to lead a normal life, but the other side of that coin is that they are accepting their restricted and troubled way of living as the norm after sixteen years. When I was fifteen years old I used to walk home with a friend from the centre of the city right through East Belfast at night. That was my normality. I couldn't, of course, do that now.

I don't think my childhood was really lonely. I did spend a lot of time on my own, of course, because I had no extended family. Ulster people are very familial, and my friends all had aunts and uncles whom they visited on Sundays – but I didn't have those things to do. On the other hand, because I enjoyed reading so much, and because I had a very lively inner mind, I always had something that I was thinking about and eventually writing about. When you are a writer, you've got to be able to spend long periods alone. I am still like that now. One part of me is sociable but the other part needs to be on my own for long stretches at a time. That is the way I have always lived. I couldn't sit in a library and write, as some of my friends do. I have to be alone and isolated.

It is difficult to have an overview of childhood. One can have an ideal picture of how you would like it to be for children – without any pressures or troubles – but the real world is not like that. I would have liked that ideal childhood for my own children, but it didn't work out for me that way. My first marriage broke up in divorce and I was on my own for a while with my three young daughters before meeting my second husband. Even so, I believe they were happy and they had a much more open childhood than I did. They had a childhood in which they met many more people, such as other writers and people in different professions. When I was growing up I didn't meet any professional people; none of my family had been to university, so I had a much narrower vision. My children grew up expecting to go to university and to travel abroad, and they did travel abroad even when they were young. To travel was a great ambition of mine, too, but I was twenty-three before I went to Europe.

When you write about your childhood you have to look at it in terms of light and dark. I can see that my childhood might sound a bit dreary to someone else, what with my father not being around very much and consequently my not having a very good relationship with him, but on the whole I was happy. I had good friends and I had my mother, with whom I got on very well. I realise that I spent a lot of my time in fantasy, daydreaming about things, and maybe that was how I coped: I built up other worlds in my head and they filled the gaps.

My childhood would, of course, have been happier had it not been cut off so abruptly by my mother's illness and death. For quite a long time afterwards I could not look back on my childhood because remembrances of her coloured it so much. But now that I can, I see it as being richly textured, woven together with the strands of friendship, my mother, the city streets, the white church, books and dreams.

# Dervla Murphy

---

Dervla Murphy was born in Co. Waterford in 1931. She fell in love with books and bicycles at a very young age and as a writer she went on to write a succession of books recalling her travels (often on a bicycle) to many exotic lands – *Full Tilt: Ireland to India with a Bicycle*, *In Ethiopia with a Mule*, *Tibetan Foothold*, *Where the Indus is Young*, *A Winter in Baltisan*, *On a Shoestring to Coorg: An Experience of Southern India* and *Eight Feet in the Andes*. Dervla Murphy has also written on topical issues such as Northern Ireland (*A Place Apart*) and the nuclear debate (*Race to the Finish? The Nuclear Stakes*) and her autobiography *Wheels within Wheels* is a candid account of her first thirty years. When not on her travels, Dervla Murphy lives in Co. Waterford.

ALTHOUGH naturally I don't remember the occasion, I associate Beethoven's Ninth Symphony with my arrival into this world. I was born in Cappoquin, Co. Waterford in a little private maternity home which was run by the local doctor. My parents lived in Lismore and as my father couldn't afford a car he walked the four miles to see me that evening, carrying with him a nine-record set of Beethoven's Ninth so that he and my mother could listen to it holding hands to celebrate my arrival. I joined in the 'Choral' Symphony with howls of pain as a result of having my bottom burned by a burst hot-water bottle.

In 1930, my father and mother had come from Dublin to Lismore, where my father took up the position of county librarian. They arrived in Lismore on their wedding-day (they couldn't afford a honeymoon) in a lorry containing all they owned in this world.

Those goods were a large golden collie named Kevin; a solid three-piece Chesterfield suite which remains as good as new to this day, apart from superficial damage inflicted by countless generations of cats; a single bed which provoked ribald comments as it was being unloaded but which seems not to have impeded progress since I was born nine and a half months later; two trunks of clothes and blankets; one tea-chest of crockery and saucepans; one cardboard carton of stainless-steel cutlery; one tea-chest of records, and a gramophone; twelve tea-chests of books; fourteen handsomely framed Arundel prints and an original surrealistic painting, by a Hindu artist, of the source of the Ganges; one inlaid Benares brass coffee-table and two silver-rimmed Georgian beer tankards; two kitchen chairs and a kitchen table with a loose leg; one round mahogany dining-table; and one very heavy black marble clock which suffered internal injuries on the journey and has never gone right since. This last item was a wedding present from our only rich relative, my mother's grand-aunt Harriet. Unluckily grand-aunt Harriet was mad as well as rich and when she died at the age of ninety-eight she left all her thousands to the Archbishop of Dublin.

*Wheels Within Wheels*

My parents were very unalike in many ways. My father came from a very republican family, whereas my mother came from a more divided lineage. She had brothers on both sides in the Civil War, while her father and grandfather would have been described as 'Dublin Castle Catholics'. They would never have questioned the right of the British to be in Ireland, but I don't think they were political at all – they just would not have thought about the matter. However, the different leanings on both sides led to a certain amount of dissension when my parents decided to get married.

Yet my father and mother did share many interests: as well as sharing a love of music and of nature – they both loved Lismore and its beautiful environs – my mother was very supportive to my father in his efforts to build up a decent library service in the county. (The previous librarian had retired leaving about nine books which were fit for circulation.)

They were both also fanatical amateur theologians. Whenever my parents took up their theological discourses, they entangled themselves in the strangest of knots, all of which bored me to infinity. In later years when my father's salary rose to a level at which he could afford a car, we would go to Dublin every other month in a little Ford 10 and these conversations would last for every mile of the 140-mile journey – a journey which took a good five hours! I used to think that there must be other parents who talked about more interesting things. But if I ever intervened in these conversations – which I occasionally did, speaking from no knowledge whatsoever – I would always be encouraged to join in. My parents were never in the least oblivious of me as a child. They welcomed my rowing in on whatever they were talking about. There was never the slightest sense of 'a child should be seen and not heard' – none of that.

I asked my mother, 'Why can't somebody teach people not to be bigots?'

'It's difficult,' she explained, 'because bigotry is self-perpetuat-ing.' (She never believed in tempering her vocabulary to the unlearned lamb.) 'Bigots are so sure they're right they don't even try to see any other point of view. But it's wrong to blame individuals for being bigoted – that's just another form of bigotry and sometimes it's worse because it's so self-righteous while pretending not to be. Usually people inherit bigotry – it's a sort of communal disease. So if you hear other children repeating non-sense about all Protestants going to hell, and so forth, don't lose your temper. Just try to make them realise that such beliefs are un-Christian and stupid. Then at least – even if they don't believe you – they'll be aware there's another point of view.'

I have never forgotten this conversation. My mother's response to my first serious querying of a widely accepted attitude had shown that in certain circumstances non-conformism was not merely allowable but desirable. At once my anxiety evaporated and I was full of happy self-importance, seeing my parents and myself as crusaders against the forces of evil.

*Wheels Within Wheels*

My father and I had, for all that, great difficulty in communi-cating with each other on any real basis. We were so alike that we knew instinctively how the other would react to a particular situation, so we felt very exposed in each other's company. It built up over the years until by the time I was fourteen there was a complete breakdown in relations between us. My rela-tionship with my mother over the years was equally complex in a different way. She was a very good-looking woman and had such tremendous charm and intellectual power that I always felt completely overshadowed by her. It wasn't her fault, but I couldn't compete in any way with her. She did everything possible to encourage my self-confidence in every way but it was just the effect of having a really remarkable woman as mother. It was inevitable I suppose that I should feel overshadowed by her.

My mother loved walking – she had met my father in Poland where she was on a walking tour and he was on a cycling tour – and she loved children – she had hoped to have six children at two-year intervals – but both interests were to be tragically cut short. When I was six months old, she became crippled with rheumatoid arthritis and by the time I was two she couldn't walk.

I can never actually remember her walking. My only recollection of her is in a bath-chair. She actually spent the best part of a year in various parts of Europe escorted by her brother in search of a cure, but there was none. By the time she returned she could not wash or dress herself or brush her beautiful long hair. My father and a maid called Nora had to tend to almost all her needs. I had an unthinking acceptance of her disability. It would have been much more difficult had I to witness her gradual incapacitation, when I was seven or eight, but as I never had any memory of her other than in a bath-chair, it just seemed to me a part of life that you really didn't think about too much. I remember her being able to feed herself when I was quite small, but by the time I was ten she had to be fed.

Despite her physical incapacitation my mother had an amazing determination to lead a normal mental life. She was tremendously enthusiastic about books – an enthusiasm she passed on to me; whenever she read a book, she would analyse it, discussing what was right with it and what was wrong with it. She had those endless theological debates with my father and she had a tremendous memory which unfortunately I haven't inherited. In a time of crisis she also developed a great talent for keeping household accounts. Her travels abroad in search of a cure for rheumatoid arthritis had left my parents in debt but my mother discovered an ability for managing money that helped to keep them afloat. I still have some of the books where she kept account of the money spent on household items.

When I was eleven I was awakened from my sleep one morning by my mother's voice, but this was a strange incoherent voice. She was drunk. I felt terribly let down and

shocked by this. Here was my mother whom I had put on a
pedestal in this degraded state. It was undoubtedly brought on
by depression at the deterioration in her health but I didn't
understand that at the time. The arthritis was becoming much
more constricting. She was now having great difficulty in
turning the pages of a book for instance – until she devised a
method of turning them with a knitting needle – but all the time
there were added pressures as she became more and more
crippled. I never let my mother know that I had seen her drunk
and eventually she overcame the problem. But I suppose if I
had not witnessed her drunken state, I would never have
realised how courageous she really was.

When I was five we moved to a house in the South Mall,
Lismore. The South Mall was Lismore's most respectable
street but this particular house hadn't been very well maintained. It was quietly falling down. It had been built in the
1820s and, being such an old house and poorly maintained,
naturally enough in a damp river valley it was falling to bits.
The plaster was regularly crumbling off the walls and I always
saw the resulting gaps as maps of strange exotic countries
which I would discover one day. The wallpaper disintegrated
when you leant against the walls, the floor boards collapsed
with dry rot and if anybody stomped around upstairs the
ceilings downstairs began to snow! There were some quaint
fittings in the house: a shower which always sprayed the
opposite wall and a lavatory whose chain was operated by
three 'morse code' pulls – long, short, long. We lived in that
house for twenty-one years, but as a child it never occurred to
me that we were living in poverty. I don't remember being cold
or hungry, nor did I feel deprived of luxuries – like a tricycle –
which other children enjoyed. After all, I had the huge,
overgrown garden and beyond that the river and the woods
and the mountains.

The previous tenant of our house had committed suicide
there – a fact which made it difficult for my parents to employ
maids. We did have a succession of these; the one I remember
best is Old Brigid. We always called her Old Brigid, even

though she was probably no older than I am now. She was with us for about four years – she died when I was nine – but those four years were a very significant part of my life. She was a sort of security symbol. She looked after me totally and did everything that needed to be done. She bathed me at seven o'clock every morning and told me fairy stories while she dried me in the airing cupboard. I never believed any of them. She could be quite strict, particularly if I threw a tantrum, but I adored her.

The other person I adored was my father's father. We called him Pappa and, apart from my parents, he was the major influence of my childhood. He was an academic – a doctor of philosophy who lectured in University College, Dublin – and very, very eccentric. He was completely unself-conscious about everything. If he felt like suddenly sitting down on the pavement and reading a book he would do just that. He loved children and he would join in with me and with other children in whatever games we played. He was blissfully unaware of time – something which I suppose attracted children to him. I never saw him as an eccentric – he was just Pappa and tremendous fun to be with. He loved books and would buy great quantities of second-hand books in the bookshops along the quays in Dublin. Every summer he used to come down to stay with us for the months of July and August. I remember jumping up and down with excitement at the railway station, waiting for his arrival. Then he would emerge from the train with a huge battered old suitcase tied with a rope and bulging with books – second-hand children's books which were 'new' to me. My joy knew no bounds.

I remember the perfection of my happiness – a perfection not often attained in this life, as I realised even then – when I woke on a dark winter's morning and switched on the light to see a tower of unread library books by my bed. From them I would look caressingly towards my own books on their shelves around the wall and reflect that now I had time to re-read; I could never decide which was the greater pleasure, re-reading old favourites or discovering new ones. For a moment I would lie still, ecstatically anticipating the day's bliss. And sometimes it would cross my mind that only Pappa could fully understand how I felt.

*Wheels Within Wheels*

What with my father being a librarian and Pappa plundering the bookshops on the Dublin quays on my behalf, I could never escape from books. Not that I wanted to. My vision of heaven was then (and still is) an infinite library. My plan for old age is to have time to sit down and re-read all the books that I want to re-read.

As a child my reading was absolutely standard: all the usual books which my generation loved – the 'William' books, *Doctor Dolittle*, *Swallows and Amazons,* etc. There was nothing advanced or precocious in my reading diet – a fact which caused my father some despair at times. He felt that I would never graduate to what he considered were books worth reading.

Being an only child didn't bother me at all. During the school holidays I loved going off alone on my bike with a few books on the carrier and finding a nice quiet place to settle down and read them. I didn't really make any close childhood friends – I preferred to live in a fantasy world a lot of the time. I had a favourite tree, a huge elm tree which I still pass every day on my way down to the river Blackwater. It is quite an extraordinary tree: very, very old, with a trunk which split into four huge branches which reached well over a hundred feet above me. I sat under that tree for hours at a time creating my own world with my teddy bears. The tree became towns and villages with families (of teddy bears) who had their own problems and clashes. I was totally involved in the bears' lives.

I also had a strange habit when I was very small of standing in the corner of a room with my hands behind my back, telling stories aloud to myself for hours and hours – stories which some visitors to the household found very alarming indeed! I had a great longing to be alone, whether in the garden or under my tree or with my books. I suppose it could have been a form of escape from the problems at home – problems which I must have been aware of to some degree.

I spent quite a lot of time entertaining what I called PITS – Private Important Thoughts. These were thoughts about death and how long I might live; what life might be like when one was fifty; what it might be like to have brothers and sisters (not that I ever wanted to have a rival in the family at all). They were, I suppose, within childish limitations, philosophical thoughts that I wouldn't ever have dreamt of mentioning to anybody.

Does every child have, as I had, an image of what adults expect children to be? And do they all courteously preserve this image, outwardly, lest their adults might be discomfited, while inwardly they are becoming something quite different, full of PITS that have nothing to do with *Doctor Dolittle* or stringing conkers? But perhaps there is something more than courtesy behind the dissembling reticence of childhood. A personality is forming and loving adults are eager to help mould it – while the child is determined to remain in control of his own evolution. Also, nothing is ready to be exposed. Most artists dislike having their incomplete work considered and discussed and this analogy, I think, is valid. The child is incomplete, too, and is constantly experimenting as he seeks his own style of thought and feeling. And all this is going on long before puberty, at an age when many children are expected still to believe in Santa Claus.

*Wheels Within Wheels*

I went, rather reluctantly, to the local national school at the age of six and a half. As someone who loved to be alone, I was unwilling to be enclosed in a schoolroom with a strange nun and strange children, but I settled in very quickly. I had already learned to read at home so I had a headstart on the others; but I turned out to be a rather lazy student.

To be honest, I was a nasty little child. I think I was very conceited in an odd sort of way. It wasn't that I thought I could do anything great, but I knew exactly what I wanted to do. I spurned all attempts to make me do subjects like maths or geography. I was only interested in English and history because I wanted to be a writer. Before I could actually physically write, I had it firmly fixed in my mind that I wanted to be a writer. I suppose books did influence that decision greatly. My whole world was centred on what I read about; books were much more important than people.

Ignoring everything except English and history naturally landed me in trouble with my teachers – none more so than Sister Andrew, with whom I had a running battle, if not a running war! I joined her class when I was eight and it was a real battle of wills. She was trying to prove that she could control a nasty little terror like me, and in the process she walloped me – physically and verbally. I was trying to prove that I could take on the adult world. We were bitter enemies for years, but in a curious way we were very fond of each other beneath all the hostility; and we have remained the best of friends throughout my adult life.

During my 'war' with Sister Andrew, I discovered that it was possible to triumph over pain. I find it hard to explain, but I managed to send a message to the painful part and control it. I did this with self-inflicted pain – such as standing in boiling water – to improve my technique, and it worked! I could detach myself totally from the pain and, to an extent, I can still do that today. At the same time, although I don't know if there is an obvious link with the pain-control, I experienced 'levitation'. I imagined that I could proceed downstairs without touching the stairs or banisters. Was that a dream or a fantasy? I am still puzzled by it, but I have since discovered it to be a fairly common experience among children. I remember reading about it in Richard Church's autobiography a few years ago. I don't know what the explanation of it is. I only know that the recollection of the feeling is very real as though it were an actual fact, but obviously it may not have been.

I was also getting an education of sorts from my father when he took me on long walks on Sunday afternoons. He would talk a great deal about natural history, astronomy and Irish history on those walks. He was very serious about educating me but I didn't in the least want to be educated.

For me, our regular Sunday afternoon walks were both physical and intellectual marathons. Week by week I would be tidily instructed about birds, or moral theology, or electricity, or Irish history, or geology, or English literature, or astronomy, or music, or agriculture, or the Renaissance. Often I wished that I were alone beneath my teddy-bear tree and then I would vindictively insulate myself against my father's voice; though to give him his due he presented all his information in carefully simple terms. Of course some of it fascinated me, despite myself, as several of his enthusiasms were by heredity my own – especially history and astronomy. On the whole, however, these didactic perambulations provided the wrong sort of fertiliser for the seed of love.

Just occasionally the barrier was lifted and we drew very close. My father had an unexpected flair for composing Learish nonsense rhymes and these charmed me utterly; when he was in one of his rare frivolous moods I would gladly have walked with him to the Giant's Causeway. Then I discovered that I had a similar flair – long since atrophied – and we enjoyed the harmony of collaboration or the stimulus of competition, each striving to outdo the other in dottiness and euphony. But the barrier always came down again at the end of these sessions, leaving us uneasily antagonistic for no discernible reason.

*Wheels Within Wheels*

My mother also contributed to my education, but she had a more subtle way of going about it. While my father was trying to persuade me to read Dickens or George Eliot, my mother would get me involved in the actual lives of these authors. She would have read a biography of George Eliot and she would tell me all about the author's life and the conditions under which she wrote. That gave me an interest in those books which my father's 'persuasion' failed to rouse.

An important part of my education was the fact that having passed the age of seven I was deemed by the Catholic Church to have reached the use of reason. I was now capable of committing sin. I took all this very seriously and went through the ritual of First Confession and First Communion.

I later came under the influence of another nun who would have us believe that sin was all about us and of course the greatest sins of all were those concerning sex. Sexual sin was repulsive but sex was never mentioned. This particular nun constantly terrorised us with moral tales.

> She was telling the 'true story' of a ten-year-old Co. Waterford girl who one day committed a filthy mortal sin (the adjective told us it was sexual) and next day fell into a stream and was drowned. Because she had not been to confession, or made an act of perfect contrition, the devil promptly dragged her soul down to hell where she was doomed to an eternity of tortures which Sister X assured us were indescribable, though she did not deter from attempting to describe them in considerable detail. None of us thought to ask our mentor the source of her information on this case. It was a cruel coincidence that I came under the influence of such an unstable woman during the unhappiest phase of my childhood.

*Wheels Within Wheels*

Every Saturday I went to confession with my classmates. I became totally scrupulous, to the extent that I kept an account of my sins in a copybook. Eventually the priest advised me to go to confession only four times a year. When I told my teacher that I would not be going to weekly confession (though I did not tell her why) she was furious. My mother noticed my unhappiness and sought the reason for it. When I told her she burst out laughing. It was a great relief to me, but she was obviously worried beneath it all and she decided that it would be better if I stopped going to Lismore school.

My mother then taught me herself for a period. She really taught me how to learn and it seemed so much more fun. The fun ended the following January when my parents decided to send me to Ring College, an Irish-speaking boarding school. This experiment proved a disaster. I was nine years old and, having led a particularly sheltered sort of life up to then, being thrown into boarding school was more than I could cope with. I was totally miserable and wrote pathetic letters to my mother to provoke her into bringing me home. I achieved this after six weeks, when I genuinely got very bad bronchitis – something to which I was prone right through my childhood.

For the next two years I stayed at home – mainly because of the difficulty in acquiring maids – and when eventually the prospect of another boarding school – the Ursuline Convent in

Waterford – loomed, I welcomed it as an escape from house-work. I enjoyed boarding school this time around. I enjoyed the anonymity of it all. It was great fun not being the centre of attention as an only child inevitably is, although that is not to say that my parents spoiled me. Both of them were quite severe disciplinarians in their different ways, but an only child is inevitably the focus of a great deal of emotional intensity and care about whether your vest is aired and socks are darned and all the rest of it. I enjoyed being free from all that and meeting such a variety of different characters.

Academically I only bothered with English and history. In those days school was much more relaxed; there wasn't the pressure for exam results that we have now, so I could get away with dodging a maths or a science class – even though I was almost expelled a few times for inattention to duty as a scholar. Looking back, I think that the teachers were very sympathetic. Obviously they couldn't condone what I was doing, but I wasn't shirking work during maths or science periods. I was in one of the music rooms doing what I always wanted to do – writing a book; so the teachers had ample evidence of what was occupying my time. There were hundreds of written pages of adventure stories of no consequence – total balderdash! – but they were practice in putting words on paper.

I eventually got into print when I won the *Cork Weekly Examiner*'s essay competition for children under sixteen. My subject was 'Picking Blackberries' and I won myself the sum of seven shillings and sixpence, which was an awful lot of money in those days. I was thrilled to see my words in print and immediately went to the library to share my triumph with my father. He was very impressed; but when I went on to win the competition for five successive weeks he decided that I should retire from that particular scene!

Although I loved to be alone with my bears and my Private Important Thoughts, I did have important friends in my childhood. One was Tommy, to whom I grew very close when I was about eight years old. He was an extraordinary little boy, whose insistence on going barefoot all year round attracted me as a kindred spirit. He was probably rather like myself, a natural 'loner'. We raided orchards together and I went to his house on Saturdays for what I thought was the most sumptuous of meals – cocoa and home-made soda bread.

Another friend was Mark. He was a neighbour and a priest, and when we first met I was five years old and he was thirty-two. Our friendship has no logical explanation whatever. The fact that he was a priest had nothing to do with it. Mark too was something of a 'loner' and he despised hypocrisy. My relationship with him was somewhat similar to my relationship with my grandfather. He was just Mark, a special person. Those who believe in reincarnation use the kind of friendship that we had as an example of a relationship that seems to have been there from the very beginning, in spite of the difference in our ages or interests or anything else. My parents, my grandfather and Mark were the four greatest influences on my life. I could discuss anything with Mark. My relationship with him was very, very deep and very constant right up until his death when I was about forty years old.

In 1944 I met a man who stayed in our house for a fortnight but even in that short period he made a great impression on me. His name was Charlie Kerins and he was an IRA man on the run, wanted for the murder of a detective in Dublin. There was a tremendous crisis of conscience in our house. My father was of a republican tradition but he was very much 'old' IRA – certainly if he were alive today he would not be a Provisional supporter – and yet it was very difficult for him to betray someone who came along and more or less threw himself on our mercy. It was a traumatic time for my parents and they felt that they had to impress on me that giving this man shelter did not imply that they were condoning what he had done.

I found Charlie to be a remarkable person and a good person. He seemed to have an extraordinary sense of certainty about what he was doing – not a fanaticism, but a sort of moral certainty that he was doing something good. His interests were very wide and I found him a marvellous companion. He was very keen on geography – a subject which had always bored me to death at school. I was interested in travel but not in what was then taught as geography. Charlie was also very knowledge-able on wild flowers and trees and was very much at one with the countryside, which also appealed to me. He stayed with us for a fortnight and then after some months he was caught. He was hanged on 1 December 1944. I was at boarding school at the time. His death wasn't as much of a shock as one might expect because my parents had been very understanding in the way they prepared me for it. Knowing Charlie as I did, I almost took it for granted that he would have been happy with his fate. That may sound odd now but that is how it seemed to me then.

For my tenth birthday I was given a present of a second-hand bicycle by my parents and an atlas by Pappa – which I suppose was an ominous sign, considering that I would spend so much of my life exploring the world on a bicycle. I recall on one of my cycling trips as a child resolving to cycle to India one day. Having consulted the atlas I discovered that there was almost no water between Ireland and India, so it would be India for me. There was no more convoluted reason than that for the original decision. But having made that decision I became very interested in India, and during my adolescence I read a lot about that country and I acquired an Indian penfriend, a Sikh girl called Mahn Kaur, with whom I corresponded for five years. Mahn Kaur's letters kindled an even greater interest in India – its people, its history and its various religions.

I loved cycling. I loved the freedom it brought and I loved exploring the beautiful countryside around Lismore. Cycling was not without its traumas, however. I set off one December morning to cycle to the top of Knockmealdown mountain, but the journey took longer than I had imagined, and on my way down a cloud came down on the mountain and I went totally astray. I spent the night in an old animal shelter and was found by a farmer the next morning. When I was eventually brought home I was quite ill and spent the next fortnight in bed. However, that experience didn't deter me. A year or so later, I cycled all the way to Helvick Head and back – a journey of fifty miles – in one day.

In the course of my travels I developed a curious interest in the dead. I would sit around on tombstones in deserted little country churchyards, thinking about the people who had died and making up stories about their families. I was also interested in the dead from an anatomical point of view. I tried to assemble a complete skeleton from the old churchyard in Lismore. At that time, the county council wasn't so strict about digging up graves and when a grave was opened for a burial, one found old bones strewn about the place – femurs, rib-cages and occasionally a skull. In fact the acquisition of a skull prevented me from completing my skeleton. I bore the skeleton home triumphantly but my father disapproved on religious grounds and ordered me to return it at once. I had never seen an actual corpse and when I did come across one, it cured me of my morbid curiosity. I came across an old vault which had been broken into and, venturing inside, I discovered that the coffins had been broken open and stripped of their lead. I almost tripped over the shrunken corpse of a woman. My courage deserted me there and then and I ran for my life. I suffered dreadful nightmares for some time after that.

During the war years it became increasingly difficult to get anybody to help out at home. I had been at boarding school for two and a half years and when I came home for the Easter holidays in 1946 my parents were on their own. I decided there and then that I would not go back to school. There was a family conference on Good Friday and three options were put to me: my parents could try to manage on their own; my mother and I could move to Dublin where I could attend day school; I could leave school and help out at home.

The ultimate decision was left to me. I chose the last option. I suppose that basically I made that decision because I didn't want my parents to be separated, but there were also guilty feelings about my performance (or non-performance) at school. It was really a 'cop-out' for me, because if I had stayed on at school I would have failed gloriously in all my exams, in every subject, probably even in English because I had never bothered to learn English grammar. (To this day I don't know what prepositions are!) It was a traumatic time for all of us. My mother was upbraided by my father's family for having put me in such a position; my father's cherished ambitions for me were no more; and my decision also drew Mark into conflict with my parents, but, of course, he still remained my friend.

For all that, the next three years (from the age of fourteen to seventeen) constituted the most exciting period of my life. Once again, books contributed greatly to that excitement. I discovered Shakespeare, for instance, whereas I had rejected having him pushed down my neck at school. It was a great joy to find out how exciting it could be to read this sort of literature instead of *Biggles* and *William* and all the others.

I discovered Shakespeare largely through Anew McMaster's travelling players. When he came to Lismore with *Hamlet*, that was really one of the highlights of my youth. I was so excited that I couldn't go home to bed. I had to cycle round the countryside for most of the night recovering from that performance.

Some people would say that my childhood hasn't ended yet! I know that I missed out on a lot of things that most children have – parties and group games, for example – but I really chose to avoid them as much as possible, just as I choose to avoid going to big parties now.

Adolescence ended for me when I fell in love for the first time at about the age of eighteen. Also at that time I went on my first cycle tour of England and Wales. I felt that I was an adult at last and I had total support from my parents. They both encouraged me to travel as much as possible, to meet new people and see new places. My travels in England also provided me with material for my first published work since the days I had won the *Cork Weekly Examiner* essay competition. My childhood ambitions were being realised. I was on my way as a writer – and soon I would be on my way to India . . .

I have no great observations to make on childhood but I do think it's true that when you meet a child and get to know him or her, twenty or thirty years later, you won't find the person will have changed all that much. I think that all the interests, all the peculiarities and all the weaknesses I have now were all there when I was a child. I don't really see any great changes in myself then and now.

# Edna O'Brien

---

Edna O'Brien was born in Co. Clare. She is the author of several novels, including *The Country Girls* trilogy, *A Pagan Place* and *Night*. Edna O'Brien has two sons and now lives in London.

I AM ALWAYS astonished by people who tell me that they don't remember their childhood, or who think there is something ridiculous or perhaps shameful about memory. We are our memories. Memory and one's dreams constitute such a bulk of what we are, because as human beings, we live very much internally.

My earliest memory is of an inability, or perhaps a fear, of getting down steps – possibly a parable for life! There were two blue stone steps leading from our back kitchen, as we called it, outside; and, as they were quite steep and I always did – indeed always do – have a longing to be out of doors, I imagine that I kept falling and having this great anxiety about having to climb to different levels.

My early memory is connected with the outdoors. It is of trees: always of trees blowing in the wind. I remember, in particular, the lustre and comfort of a copper beech behind our house. I also have an indoor memory – which I think most children have – of the bedroom being a long way from where one's parents were. There was, if you like, a sense of banishment, of being cut off. It is a memory that goes back quite a long way: I remember being in my cot and feeling stranded in it. I am told, and it is something that I believe, that the earlier you remember, the better for yourself, the more you are in touch with yourself. I know that when I start to write, my memories come to me unsummoned and I remember things – a piece of wallpaper, a stain in a flower in the wallpaper, the way the sun came in on the linoleum, the dust in the room – and once I start remembering, I can't stop.

Home was in Tuamgraney, Co. Clare. I was the youngest of four children (I had one brother and two sisters) although there had been a child before me that had died, so I was the fifth child really. I was a good deal younger than the sister who was next to me so that when my brother and sisters went away to school for much of the time I was the only child at home with my parents.

My relationship with my father wasn't very serene. It got better, of course, as he got older and as I grew older and understood him more; but he was a very restless man. He had been married very young, at twenty-three or -four, which is young – even though people do get married nowadays at that age. I didn't feel easy with him. I was afraid of him; and really, I think, chemically we were not elective creatures. I read once in Herzen's memoirs that the relationships we form with people – whether we love or don't love them – are always chemical; but the fact that people happen to be your parents or your brother or your sisters doesn't necessarily mean that they are the people in the world to whom you're the closest. It would be humbug to pretend that. If you are close to them, then it's an extra bonus from God. I was afraid of my father, and I would be a hypocrite if I said that it had been an easy or a loving relationship.

I miss very much not having had a tender relationship with him, but you have to measure the blessings as much as the curses; I feel that to a great extent it was obviously that tension and that fear that were the sources of my becoming a writer. I don't think happy people become writers. They wouldn't bother, because writing by necessity is a very gruelling and very lonely and very anxious occupation – that's if you take it seriously. I have also to thank my father for something else which I remember very clearly: that is a great sense of story-telling. He was a hypnotic story-teller, and I was very aware of that, but he was an egotistical man and he didn't want any interruptions in his stories. He loved it when visitors came because then he could tell again the stories that he had told before.

He was also a gambler. He loved playing cards, he liked

greyhounds and he loved horses. My mother was not approving of horses, but even so there always seemed to be very restless unwieldy thoroughbreds – usually roan-coloured – in the fields. I was quite afraid of them: I remember them being broken in – and that is quite a violent thing. But my father loved these horses.

He also loved a drink and he was unlucky in that he couldn't drink very much without it having a disastrous effect on him, and on us.

I was very close to my mother. I have written about her in a story called 'A Rose in the Heart', in which the child describes her mother as being *everything* – the tabernacle with the host in it, the altar with the flowers, the bog with the bog lakes, the cupboard with the linen. My mother was someone to whom I felt umbilically and osmotically attached. I remember that when I was going to school each morning, I was terrified that she would not be there when I came home. It was very childish, I suppose; but it was a question of distance – the school was only one and a half miles away, but to a fearful child it was almost an eternity.

We lived in a big house – or so it seemed to me as a child – with about five bedrooms. There was a long avenue up from the roadside gate, then a second gate that led into the front of the house; and when the sun shone I used to think that it was a kind of heaven. It was a very beautiful place.

> Standing on the stone step to look across the fields I felt, as I always did, that rush of freedom and pleasure when I looked at all the various trees and the outer stone buildings set far away from the house, and at the fields very green and very peaceful. Outside the paling wire was a walnut tree, and under its shade there were bluebells, tall and intensely blue, a grotto of heaven – blue flowers among the limestone boulders. And my swing was swaying in the wind, and all the leaves on all the treetops were stirring lightly.

*The Country Girls*

My mother was extremely house-proud. In a sense, the house was done up like a doll's house. My mother had a wonderful collection of china objects. I remember in particular a pair of large busts of ladies, called Iris and Gala. My mother would dust them, put an artificial flower in the hand of one of them – and paint their finger nails! She was also very keen on furniture. Whenever she had the money, she would go to auctions and buy something new; and as a result the rooms were crammed with furniture.

Oddly enough, the room I remember best was called the 'vacant' room – because it was still relatively devoid of furniture. It had a huge long oak table, which in autumn was laden down with ripening apples. There are two things I connect with that room – the smell of slightly rotting apples and the fact that the wallpaper was hung upside down! The latter event happened many, many years ago on a day when my mother had gone to Limerick. She had a penchant for fortune tellers, and when she visited one in Limerick she was told that there was a job being done in her house that day and it would be done wrong. She came home to discover that the wallpaper motif was cockeyed. It had been hung upside down. She was furious.

Sometimes we would visit my grandparents, who lived five miles away. I remember once walking there, or rather refusing to walk when I grew tired, and my poor mother had to carry me. I have written a story which is located in that house. It's called 'My Mother's Mother'.

I loved my mother, but yet I was glad when the time came to go to her mother's house each summer. It was a little house in the mountains and it commanded a fine view of the valley and the great lake below. From the front door, glimpsed through a pair of very old binoculars, one could see the entire Shannon Lake studded with various islands. On a summer's day this was a thrill. I would be put standing on a kitchen chair, while someone held the binoculars, and sometimes I marvelled, though I could not see at all, as the lenses had not been focused properly. The sunshine made everything better and though we were not down by the lake, we imagined dipping our feet in it, or seeing people in boats fishing and then stopping to have a picnic. We imagined lake water lapping.

*Returning*

It was a humbler house than ours, a cottage really. It had a hearth fire with a salt hole in the wall near the fire to keep the salt dry. I remember one evening when my grandparents started to tease me, telling me that my mother was not my real mother. I didn't believe them at first, of course; but when they persisted I became so frenzied that I actually had a fit. They had to mollify me with blancmange and pieces of porter cake.

And of course that is the other thing about childhood that sticks in the mind – the food! I always had a hankering for sweet things and shop things. Trifle, in particular, stays in my mind because it would be put to set the night before in a bowl and laid on a tiled floor to cool. Of course I would come down early in the morning and steal a bit of it.

We lived in a quiet farming area where, as I have described elsewhere, nothing much happened to disturb the passage of the seasons. Strangely enough, I remember only two seasons from my childhood. In summer, I remember picking wild flowers on (what seemed then) the very long and very precarious journey to the village school. In winter, I remember the tall, frosted grass, like plumes of ostrich, and the trees, fields – everything fixed in that bejewelled frost-like limbo.

> Born and bred in a townland that bordered on other townlands of equal indistinctiveness. Fairly arable land, tillage in some fields, potatoes in most, potatoes sprayed twice a year and consequently the leaves bright as peacocks' plumage until the rain came and washed the copper sulphate away. During the summer one saw from any window the dock and the ragwort, rampant, high, and submerged in the grasses some old piece of rusted farm machinery and sometimes a fox making its way swiftly to the hen house. There were nice dozy hens, a sow, and to everyone's trepidation one reigning bull in some field or farmyard to which were brought all the resisting brown cows of the neighbourhood.
>
> *Mother Ireland*

'Life was fervid, enclosed, catastrophic,' that passage continues. It was religiously very fervid: religion permeated every aspect of one's life. My mind was never not on the question – was I or was I not committing sin?

In *The Country Girls*, Kate is an only child – and indeed when my brother and sisters were away I felt like an only child – but she has an *alter ego* in the form of her best friend, Baba, who is outrageous and the opposite to everything that one would like to be. I think I was a very devout and a very good child and in a sense never dared to do wrong. I was very keen on fasting and punishments. One of the punishments I visited upon myself was to gargle with salt water at the rain barrel outside the house. This I thought would keep me 'in' with God and my parents, but obviously churning away inside this good girl was the subversive character of Baba. She is not a person, but simply the other side of what it means to be good.

We said the rosary every night, of course, but along with that I was getting in and out of bed every five minutes to say more prayers and ejaculations. The fear of hell – and indeed of purgatory – was outlandish and it was pervasive. I remember reading in St Admanan, I think, a version of the after-life which makes Dante's *Inferno* jocular. It described waiting for hell in the next world in an utter, utter wilderness. There were different bridges leading to banishment. If you weren't an utter sinner you crossed on a bridge that was fairly level; but if you had been dissolute in your life, you began on a wider bridge that grew narrower and narrower until you were sucked into the flames. The description of your tongue turning into flame and then the flame inhabiting your brain was terrifying. It was a totally destructive attitude to the after-life. I hope there isn't one.

Life was enclosed in the way that any village is enclosed. Everybody knew our life and we knew everyone else's life. If somebody had shingles, if somebody got consumption, if somebody brought a cow to the fair and didn't sell – you always knew. I remember the great confusion and upset that ensued when we sold a cow in calf and about three days later the purchaser came back, outraged, to say that the cow was not in calf. In fact, the cow had calved without anyone knowing it and the calf was later found stillborn in some bushes. But such was our world that the whole countryside knew about the row.

Life was catastrophic. The sense of catastrophe is peculiar to a lot of Irish people. I was always nervous of something that would befall one. It was a sense of not being physically at ease in one's body and feeling that one would fall or drown or come to grief. As a result I am ashamed to say that I don't drive a car – and I wouldn't call myself a wonderful bicycle-rider either!

I had fears of animals – which is a great handicap when you live in the country. I was frightened by the people around me. I identify very much with Kafka in that respect. Dogs were a source of terror to me. They were so unpredictable; they would take fits; and I remember being badly bitten on the neck by a dog, trying desperately to escape and thinking I never would.

Also, of course, there was the fact of our own history – what one was taught and what one read at school was dinned into one as the catastrophic story of what had happened to our country.

I remember the travelling players coming to our village. When the Shannon Players came it was a great event because they brought that much-sought and much-valued word, 'glamour', to the village. Their coming was always announced with great ceremony beforehand, but in fact the repertoire was usually the same: *East Lynne* and *Murder in the Red Barn*. There would be a comedy sketch first, then a raffle and then a play. I can still see the Village Hall, with black curtains over the windows and six paraffin lamps which served as footlights at the front of the stage. And on the stage those characters looked so real in their pancake make-up. I think that no theatre I ever attended in my grown-up life could assume the awe and the magic that I felt then in that little village hall.

Living as we did a bit 'over the fields', my brother and sisters and I were always longing for people to come. One regular occasion for meeting people was threshing day, when work-men from all around came to help out. We children were not really included – except to butter the bread and bring up tea to the men every ten minutes (or so it seemed) – but it was still a great and exciting event for us.

The other great event was Christmas and I connect it very much with things my mother would be doing. She was a very generous woman, and she was forever making Christmas cakes for various people, especially for the nuns. When it came to icing the cakes she did it with such a flourish that I felt she was Leonardo Da Vinci. She would do boiled icing and then work on it with great pride, with a spatula, making dents and elevations and finally decorating it with little silver balls.

When we killed a pig, which was about twice a year – a pretty gory event – my mother would give away fillets of pork and we loved going to each house because we got lots of praise – and maybe even sixpence.

The national school I attended was a bit 'shambolical', as Sean O'Casey might say. Our teacher was a very moody and a very nervy creature. Sometimes she would be very pleasant to you and you would be her favourite; and then, regardless of having done anything to alter the situation, you'd be a stooge – somebody to be victimised. So schooling was erratic, to say the least.

There were happy moments – especially when we read literature. Thoreau was one of my favourites, and Leigh Hunt, too. I was always in love with language – and with art, which I still believe is the one really profound religion for mankind. The only books I had access to were school books. There were very good extracts in them that I still remember – bits of Leigh Hunt, poems by Shelley and so on.

There were no books at all in our house. My mother was extremely suspicious of literature because she thought it was bad and could lead to sin. My father wasn't interested in books. His reading was confined to the *Irish Field* and bloodstock manuals. There was no travelling library in our locality then. There were simply no books. Once, when someone in the village actually got a copy of *Rebecca*, there was such an avidity for it that it was loaned by the page. Unfortunately you would get page 84 and then page 103. As a result, I did not grasp the story of *Rebecca* for ages. But however restricted the diet may have been, reading was and still is my great prop against reality. As Mr Eliot says, human kind cannot bear too much reality!

When I left national school I went to a convent boarding school in Loughrea, Co. Galway. A lot of my life there was as portrayed in *The Country Girls* – certainly the actual bleakness of the convent and the regimented life found their way into that book. But the narrative is not true: I was not expelled. I was a good student and keen on learning. I suppose I did have the inevitable thoughts of a vocation – most convent girls do; you fall in love with nuns and you think how beautiful it would be to devote your life to the service of God. Looking back on it, though, it was just a whim – there was nothing serious in it. When *The Country Girls* was published, the head nun wrote me a rather crisp letter about my 'wicked book'. 'I give credence an open mind until I read it,' she said. I never heard what she made of it when she did read it – that is, if ever she did.

When I finished boarding school I went to Dublin to be a pharmacist.

> Goodbye to the humble little mounds, the ragwort, the chicken run, the dozy hens, goodbye to the tillage, goodbye to the green gate with its intractable hasp, goodbye to the ghosts wherein were contained all seeds of future laughter, skittishness and woe. Goodbye to the ineradicable past.
>
> Dublin was where I veered towards and eventually I got there, arriving by train, the suitcase reinforced with twine, the head full of fancy; conceiving of my destiny as being like that of a heroine who, upon being brought from Munster, faded in the city 'for consumption has no pity for blue eyes and golden hair'.

*Mother Ireland*

On my very first night in Dublin, my sister took me down O'Connell Street. It was like being in Mecca – with all the lights and a flashing Bovril sign. No stars in the heavens shone like those city lights. I lost all interest in nature when I first came to the city. I worked very hard, serving my apprenticeship in a chemist's shop on the Cabra Road by day, and attending lectures and studying by night. I always say that I learned to cook while working in that chemist's shop, because we made our own medicines: emulsions, tablets, suppositories – we made them all. And all the time, even though I was working extremely hard, I would find time to write articles – of a very cretinous nature I'm sure! – because I was determined to be a writer. There was no time for leisure – and no money anyway. The thought of being able to afford an ice-cream, or to go to the cinema or a stage show, was way beyond me.

I think one is born a writer. I know that circumstances alter the subject of one's fiction, but the writing is there from the beginning, all the same. It is somehow that living is incomplete until it is fastened through words into a piece of fiction or drama. I always knew that I would be a writer – for as long as I can remember I knew that I would write. I didn't know what it meant to be a writer but I knew that my reality, my life and my fate would be lived out through words: 'In the beginning was the Word . . .'

I wrote a novel when I was eight or nine. I wish I still had it because it could only be hilarious! I can't remember what I called it; but it was a story of a blacksmith's daughter who was very wretched and made to work very hard in the forge. One day the gypsies came and the girl fell in love with one of them and eloped with him. It was a bit like *Lord Ullan's Daughter*, except that the gypsy turned out to be a bad egg and there was a great search for him across the country. I wrote it in a copybook and hid it in a trunk. Years later I learnt that the Brontës had written little stories as children but wisely they had kept theirs. Mine was simply lost or thrown out; I always thought I would refind it but I never did.

In my mind I still live in the locality of my early childhood and when I write I do so with the greatest ease when I set stories there. I am not 'cataloguing' the people of the village – my writing is an imaginative re-inventing of those people. If *they* were to write their stories, they would write differently. My characters are spectres of reality, if you like. If you look at Jack Yeats's painting of, say, *West of Ireland Horse-dealers*, you will notice how he coats them with his strange vivid blue

lunatic colours; that is Jack Yeats's 're-inventing' of his characters, if you like. I would think that my 'colour' veers between
red and black – because I have that sense of darkness and also a
sense of vividness.

The characters in my stories, particularly in *Returning*, are
very colourful. I was drawing on very early conceptions of
people in that book, but I then had to bring the story 'up to
date', because a child's view is naturally limited. A child
looking up at its father or its mother sees a monumental
statuesque figure; and it's the same when looking at them
emotionally. Perhaps this passage from one of the stories, 'The
Doll', will illustrate how I was trying to take an early association and contrast it, or link it, with one's present self and all
that one has learned, or half-learned, or not learned at all.

Walking down the street, where I walk in memory, morning noon
and night, I could not tell what it was, precisely, that reduced me to
such wretchedness. Indeed it was not death but rather the gnawing
conviction of not having yet lived. All I could tell was that the stars
were as singular and as wondrous as I remembered them and that
they still seemed like a link, an enticement to the great heavens, and
that one day I would reach them and be absorbed into their glory,
and pass from a world that, at that moment, I found to be rife with
cruelty and stupidity, a world that had forgotten how to give.

'Tomorrow...', I thought. 'Tomorrow I shall be gone', and
realised that I had not lost the desire to escape or the strenuous
habit of hoping.

*Returning*

There were some marvellous things in my childhood. I was
very blessed as a child and had a great inner life. I talked to the
trees and I had a great love of both nature and language. I could
have had a happier childhood, perhaps, but it was by no means
joyless. My life has had terror and some dramatic things in it,
but it has also been full of rapture about many things, particularly about love and landscape.

Those lanes, byres, fields, flowers, insects, suns, moons and stars
are forever reoccurring and tantalising me with a possibility of a

golden key which would lead beyond birth to the roots of one's lineage.

*Mother Ireland*

I think that nothing ends. In fact, I have written about that very thing in a story where the child remembers 'the little stream that went "tra la la" and the clouds and that far off childhood region where no one ever dies, not even oneself'. I don't think that childhood ends. I think that the people in this world who lose touch with their childhood have lost something really intrinsic and crucial. It is hard to hold on to it in the hard, realistic world in which we live – much more materialistic than it was twenty years ago – a world in which the interest in literature is very marginal. (Most bestsellers are books that I certainly can't read. Bilge. They have nothing to do with literature! They are irrelevant.)

I hope that I have not lost my childhood sensibilities and I hope that I never will, because it is the fount and source of my writing.